ATLAS OF

SKELETAL

MUSCLES

SECOND EDITION

ATLAS OF SKELETAL MUSCLES

SECOND EDITION

ROBERT J. STONE
Suffolk Community College

JUDITH A. STONE
Suffolk Community College

WCB **Wm. C. Brown Publishers**

Dubuque, IA Bogota Boston Buenos Aires Caracas Chicago Guilford, CT
London Madrid Mexico City Seoul Singapore Sydney Taipei Tokyo Toronto

Project Team

Editor *Colin Wheatley*
Developmental Editor *Kristine Noel*
Production Editor *Kay J. Brimeyer*
Marketing Manager *Tom Lyon*
Designer *Barbara J. Hodgson*
Advertising Coordinator *Heather Wagner*

 Wm. C. Brown Publishers

President and Chief Executive Officer *Beverly Kolz*
Vice President, Director of Editorial *Kevin Kane*
Vice President, Sales and Market Expansion *Virginia S. Moffat*
Vice President, Director of Production *Colleen A. Yonda*
Director of Marketing *Craig S. Marty*
National Sales Manager *Douglas J. DiNardo*
Executive Editor *Michael D. Lange*
Advertising Manager *Janelle Keeffer*
Production Editorial Manager *Renée Menne*
Publishing Services Manager *Karen J. Slaght*
Royalty/Permissions Manager *Connie Allendorf*

 A Times Mirror Company

Copyright © 1997 Times Mirror Higher Education Group, Inc.
All rights reserved

Library of Congress Catalog Card Number: 96–77566

Cover design by Schneck-DePippo graphics

ISBN 0–697–13790–2

Printed in the United States of America by Times Mirror Higher Education Group, Inc.,
2460 Kerper Boulevard, Dubuque, IA 52001

10 9 8 7 6 5 4 3 2 1

DEDICATION

To Karen, Andrew, and Laura for their interest,
enthusiasm, and cooperation.

CONTENTS

PREFACE

This book is a study guide to the anatomy and actions of human skeletal muscles. It is designed for use by students of physical therapy, chiropractic, medicine, nursing, physical education, and other health-related fields. It also serves as a compact reference for the practicing professional.

The first chapter presents labeled line drawings of the skeleton, which include all structures that are used in describing origins and insertions in the later chapters. A master numbering system is used so that each structure is labeled with the same number in all drawings.

The second chapter describes the various movements of the body.

In chapters three through nine the origin, insertion, action, and innervation of the skeletal muscles are described and each muscle is presented on a separate page with a line drawing. The spinal cord level of the nerve fibers that innervate each muscle are included in parentheses after the name of each nerve.

The drawings include the following important features:

1. Bones and cartilage containing muscle attachment sites are shaded.
2. Adjacent structures are shown.
3. Muscle fibers are drawn by direction.
4. Muscle fibers are shown on the undersurface of bone and cartilage as dashed lines.
5. Tendons and aponeuroses are shown.

These features aid in visual orientation and understanding of the action of the muscles.

Since our primary goal is to describe the muscles moving the skeleton we have not described the muscles of the perineum, eye, tympanic cavity, tongue, larynx, pharynx, or palate.

Several new features have been added to the second edition. Notes have been included on many pages to show how muscles are used. Relationships among many of the muscles have also been indicated where appropriate. Thirteen new labeled drawings of the major muscle groups are presented throughout chapters three to nine.

Much of the text has been rewritten to increase precision and clarity.

We extend our appreciation to Mr. George Boykin, the jolly proprietor of the gross anatomy laboratories at the Health Sciences Center of the State University of New York at Stony Brook, for his help and encouragement over the years. We also thank Mr. Vincent Verdisco and Ms. Diane Chandler for their technical advice with the artwork, Ms. Katherine Juner for her secretarial services, and the following list of reviewers: S. R. Peterson, University of Alberta; Sherwin Mizell, Indiana University; Danielle Desroches, William Paterson College; Michael R. Hawes, The University of Calgary; Farica R. Bialstock, Nassau Community College; and Robert J. Gurney, Grant MacEwan College.

Robert J. Stone

Judith A. Stone

List of Reviewers

C. David Bridges
Purdue University

Christopher C. Chabot
Plymouth State College

Jeanne M. Foley
Michigan State University

John H. Langdon
University of Indianapolis

Bob Lehnberg
Carolina School of Massage Therapy

Nancy C. Lovell
University of Alberta

Stephen Nawrocki
University of Indianapolis

James A. Rankin
University of Calgary

Polly Phillips-Sanborn
Miami-Dade Community College

Albert L. Threlfall
Pikes Peak Community College

CHAPTER ONE
THE SKELETON

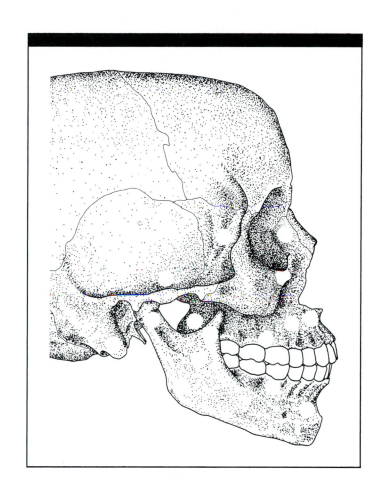

BONES OF THE SKULL—LATERAL VIEW

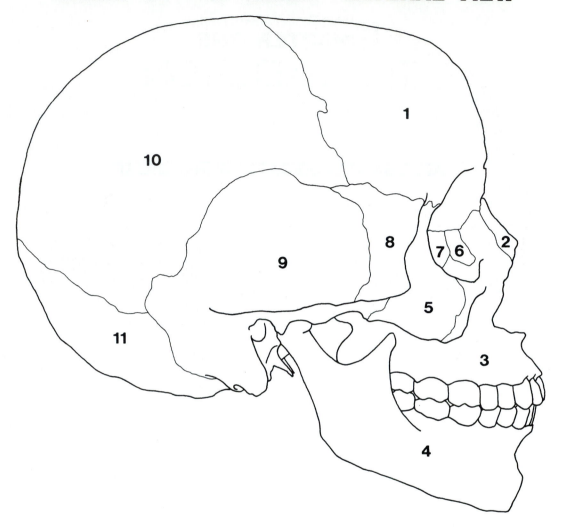

1. Frontal
2. Nasal
3. Maxilla
4. Mandible
5. Zygomatic

6. Lacrimal
7. Ethmoid
8. Sphenoid
9. Temporal
10. Parietal
11. Occipital

SKULL—LATERAL VIEW

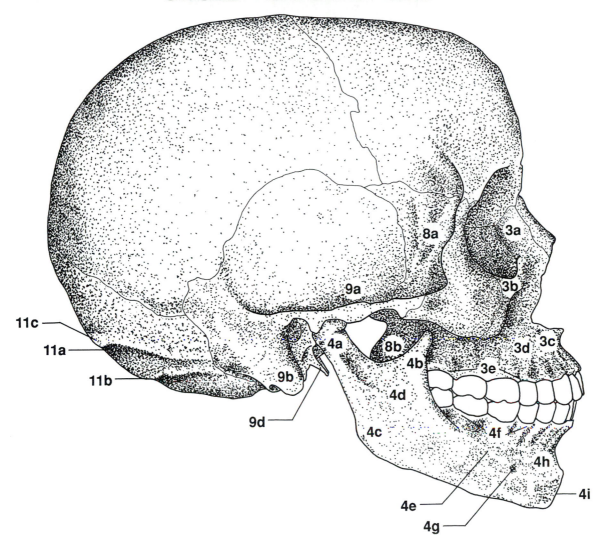

3a. Frontal process (maxilla)	**4g.** Mental foramen (mandible)
3b. Zygomatic process (maxilla)	**4h.** Incisive fossa of mandible
3c. Incisive fossa of maxilla	**4i.** Symphysis of mandible
3d. Canine fossa (maxilla)	**8a.** Greater wing of sphenoid bone
3e. Alveolar border of maxilla	**8b.** Lateral pterygoid plate
4a. Neck of condyle (mandible)	**9a.** Temporal fossa
4b. Coronoid process (mandible)	**9b.** Mastoid process (temporal bone)
4c. Angle of the mandible	**9d.** Styloid process (temporal bone)
4d. Ramus (mandible)	**11a.** Superior nuchal line (occipital bone)
4e. Oblique line (mandible)	**11b.** Inferior nuchal line (occipital bone)
4f. Alveolar border of mandible	**11c.** External occipital protuberance

Note: The zygomatic arch is formed by the zygomatic process of the temporal bone meeting the zygomatic bone.

SKULL—LATERAL VIEW

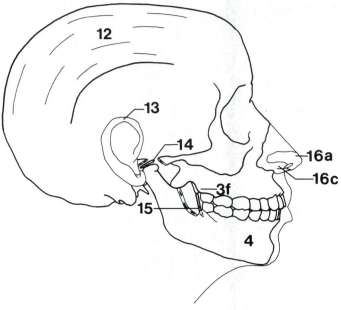

3f. Tuberosity of maxilla
4. Mandible
12. Galea aponeurotica
13. Helix of ear
14. Articular disk of temporomandibular joint
15. Pterygomandibular raphe
16a. Greater alar cartilage
16c. Ala

SKULL—POSTERIOR VIEW

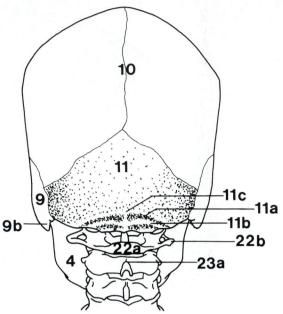

4. Mandible
9. Temporal bone
9b. Mastoid process (temporal bone)
10. Parietal bone
11. Occipital bone
11a. Superior nuchal line (occipital bone)
11b. Inferior nuchal line (occipital bone)
11c. External occipital protuberance
22a. Posterior arch of atlas
22b. Transverse process of atlas
23a. Spinous process of axis

SKULL—ANTERIOR VIEW

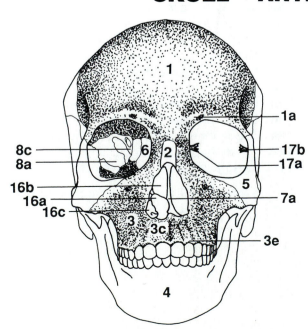

1. Frontal bone
1a. Superciliary arch (frontal bone)
2. Nasal bone
3. Maxilla
3c. Incisive fossa of maxilla
3e. Alveolar border of maxilla
4. Mandible
5. Zygomatic bone
6. Lacrimal bone
7a. Nasal septum
8a. Greater wing of sphenoid bone
8c. Lesser wing of sphenoid bone
16a. Greater alar cartilage
16b. Nasal cartilage
16c. Ala
17a. Medial palpebral ligament
17b. Lateral palpebral raphe (ligament)

SKULL TO HUMERUS—LATERAL VIEW

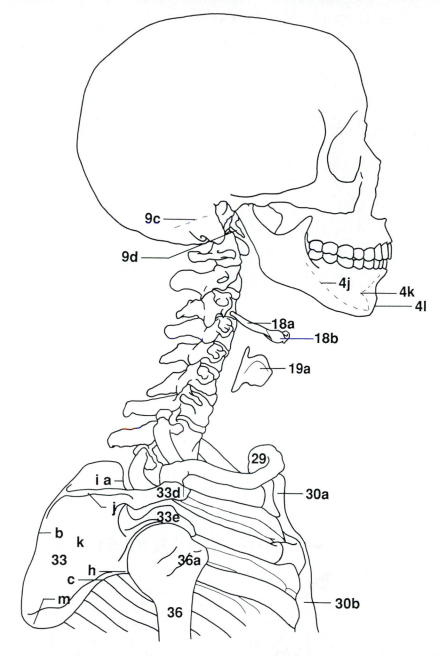

4j. Mylohyoid line (medial surface of mandible)	**33a.** Superior border of scapula
4k. Inferior mental spine (inner surface of mandible)	**33b.** Vertebral (medial) border of scapula
4l. Symphysis of mandible	**33c.** Axillary (lateral) border of scapula
9c. Mastoid notch (medial surface of temporal bone)	**33d.** Acromion (scapula)
9d. Styloid process (temporal bone)	**33e.** Coracoid process (scapula)
18a. Greater cornu of hyoid	**33h.** Infraglenoid tubercle (scapula)
18b. Body of hyoid	**33i.** Supraspinous fossa (scapula)
19a. Lamina of thyroid cartilage	**33j.** Crest of spine (scapula)
29. Clavicle	**33k.** Infraspinous fossa (scapula)
30a. Manubrium	**33m.** Inferior angle of scapula
30b. Body of sternum	**36.** Humerus
33. Scapula	**36a.** Greater tuberosity of humerus

SKULL TO STERNUM—ANTERIOR VIEW

(Mandible and maxilla removed)

11. Occipital bone	**22c.** Anterior arch of atlas
11d. Jugular process of occipital bone	**23.** Axis
20a. Transverse process of vertebra	**31a.** Scalene tubercle of first rib
	31b. Second rib

RIB CAGE, PECTORAL GIRDLE, UPPER ARM—ANTERIOR VIEW

(Ribs partially removed, right arm disarticulated)

29. Clavicle	**33l.** Subscapular fossa (scapula)
30. Sternum	**36.** Humerus
30a. Manubrium	**36a.** Greater tuberosity (tubercle) of humerus
30c. Xiphoid process	**36b.** Lesser tuberosity of humerus
31c. Tubercle of rib	**36c.** Intertubercular (bicipital) groove (humerus)
31d. Angle of rib	**36d.** Deltoid tuberosity (humerus)
32. Costal cartilage	**37a.** Radial tuberosity (radius)
33. Scapula	**38a.** Ulnar tuberosity (ulna)
33d. Acromion (scapula)	**38b.** Coronoid process (ulna)
33e. Coracoid process (scapula)	**92.** Lateral lumbocostal arch
33f. Supraglenoid tubercle (scapula)	**93.** Medial lumbocostal arch

SKELETON—POSTERIOR VIEW

(Enlargement of lumbar vertebrae)

20a. Transverse process of vertebra
20b. Spinous process of vertebra
20c. Mamillary process of vertebra
20d. Accessory process of vertebra
24. Ligamentum nuchae
25. Supraspinous ligaments
26a. Lateral sacral crest
26b. Sacral foramina
26c. Medial sacral crest
29. Clavicle
31c. Tubercle of rib
31d. Angle of rib
33. Scapula
33d. Acromion (scapula)
36. Humerus
37. Radius
38. Ulna
38c. Olecranon process (ulna)
52a. Posterior superior iliac spine
52b. Iliac crest

RIGHT ARM—POSTERIOR VIEW

34. Radial collateral ligament
35. Annular ligament
36. Humerus
36e. Lateral supracondylar ridge (humerus)
36f. Lateral epicondyle (humerus)
37. Radius
37c. Dorsal tubercle (radius)
37d. Styloid process (radius)
38. Ulna
38c. Olecranon process (ulna)
39. Interosseous membrane
40. Scaphoid (navicular)
41. Lunate
43. Trapezium
44. Trapezoid
45. Capitate
46. Hamate
47. Triquetrum
48. Metacarpals
49a. Proximal phalanges
49b. Middle phalanges
49c. Distal phalanges

RIGHT ARM
ANTERIOR VIEW

RIGHT HAND
ANTERIOR VIEW

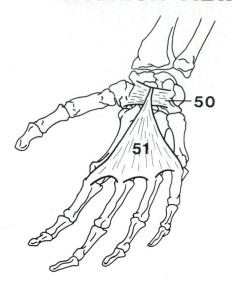

34. Radial collateral ligament
35. Annular ligament
36. Humerus
36g. Medial supracondylar ridge (humerus)
36h. Medial epicondyle (humerus)
37. Radius
37b. Pronator tuberosity (radius)
38. Ulna
38b. Coronoid process (ulna)
38c. Olecranon process (ulna)
38d. Supinator crest (ulna)
39. Interosseous membrane
40a. Tubercle of scaphoid (navicular)
41. Lunate
42. Pisiform
43a. Tubercle of trapezium
44. Trapezoid
45. Capitate
46a. Hook of hamate
47. Triquetrum
48. Metacarpals
49a. Proximal (first) phalanges
49b. Middle (second) phalanges
49c. Distal (third) phalanges
50. Flexor retinaculum
51. Palmar aponeurosis

LUMBAR AND PELVIC REGION—ANTERIOR VIEW

20a. Transverse process of vertebra
20e. Body of vertebra
21. Intervertebral disk
26d. Second sacral vertebra
26e. Third sacral vertebra
26f. Fourth sacral vertebra
26g. Ala of sacrum
52e. Anterior superior iliac spine
52f. Anterior inferior iliac spine
52g. Iliac fossa
52h. Arcuate line (ilium)
52i. Iliopectineal eminence (ilium)
53a. Ramus of ischium
54a. Superior ramus of pubis
54b. Inferior ramus of pubis
54c. Pubic crest
54d. Pubic symphysis
54e. Pubic tubercle
55. Greater sciatic notch
56. Sacrotuberous ligament
57. Obturator foramen
59. Inguinal ligament
60. Superior pubic ligament
61. Iliolumbar ligament
62. Rectus sheath
65. Linea alba
68. Femur
68a. Greater trochanter (femur)
68b. Trochanteric fossa (femur)
68c. Lesser trochanter (femur)

PELVIC GIRDLE TO KNEE LATERAL VIEW

52c
52b
52e

68

67

72

74c

THORACIC TO PELVIC REGION LATERAL VIEW

(Arm and leg removed)

33g

32

65

64

66

52d

59

63

32. Costal cartilage
33g. Glenoid cavity (scapula)
52d. Anterior iliac crest
59. Inguinal ligament
63. Acetabulum
64. Thoracolumbar fascia
65. Linea alba
66. Abdominal aponeurosis

52b. Iliac crest
52c. Iliac tubercle
52e. Anterior superior iliac spine
67. Iliotibial tract
68. Femur
72. Synovial membrane of knee joint
74c. Lateral condyle of tibia

PELVIC GIRDLE—POSTERIOR VIEW

52. Ilium
53a. Ramus of ischium
53b. Ischial tuberosity
53c. Spine of ischium
54g. Body of pubis
57. Obturator foramen
58. Obturator membrane
68a. Greater trochanter (femur)
68d. Intertrochanteric crest (femur)
68f. Quadrate line (femur)

PELVIC GIRDLE AND UPPER LEG THREE-QUARTER POSTERIOR VIEW

26. Sacrum
27. Aponeurosis of erector spinae
28. Coccyx
52b. Iliac crest
52j. Posterior gluteal line (ilium)
52k. Middle (anterior) gluteal line (ilium)
52l. Inferior gluteal line (ilium)
56. Sacrotuberous ligament
68a. Greater trochanter (femur)
68g. Gluteal tuberosity (femur)
68h. Linea aspera (femur)

PELVIC GIRDLE TO LEG—ANTERIOR VIEW

52. Ilium
52e. Anterior superior iliac spine
52f. Anterior inferior iliac spine
54b. Inferior ramus of pubis
54f. Pectineal line (pubis)
54g. Body of pubis
68. Femur
68a. Greater trochanter (femur)
68c. Lesser trochanter (femur)
68e. Intertrochanteric line (femur)
68i. Lateral supracondylar line (femur)
68j. Medial supracondylar line (femur)
69. Quadriceps tendon
70. Patella
71. Patellar ligament
74. Tibia
74a. Tuberosity of tibia

PELVIC GIRDLE TO LEG—POSTERIOR VIEW

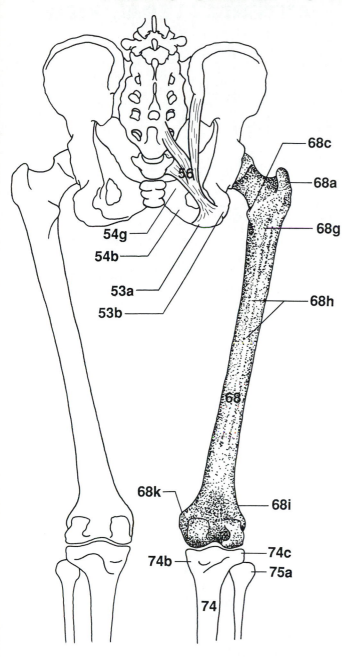

53a. Ramus of ischium
53b. Ischial tuberosity
54b. Inferior ramus of pubis
54g. Body of pubis
56. Sacrotuberous ligament
68. Femur
68a. Greater trochanter (femur)
68c. Lesser trochanter (femur)
68g. Gluteal tuberosity (femur)
68h. Linea aspera (femur)
68i. Lateral supracondylar line (femur)
68k. Adductor tubercle (femur)
74. Tibia
74b. Medial condyle of tibia
74c. Lateral condyle of tibia
75a. Head of fibula

RIGHT LEG
ANTEROLATERAL VIEW

RIGHT FOOT
ANTEROLATERAL VIEW

- **68.** Femur
- **74.** Tibia
- **74c.** Lateral condyle of tibia
- **75.** Fibula
- **76.** Interosseous membrane
- **77.** Lateral talocalcaneal ligament
- **78.** Inferior extensor retinaculum
- **83.** Talus
- **84.** Calcaneus
- **85.** Navicular
- **86.** Medial cuneiform
- **87.** Intermediate cuneiform
- **88.** Lateral cuneiform
- **89.** Cuboid
- **90.** Metatarsal bones
- **90a.** First metatarsal
- **90b.** Second metatarsal
- **90c.** Third metatarsal
- **90d.** Fourth metatarsal
- **90e.** Fifth metatarsal
- **91a.** Proximal phalanges
- **91b.** Middle phalanges
- **91c.** Distal phalanges

RIGHT LEG—POSTERIOR VIEW

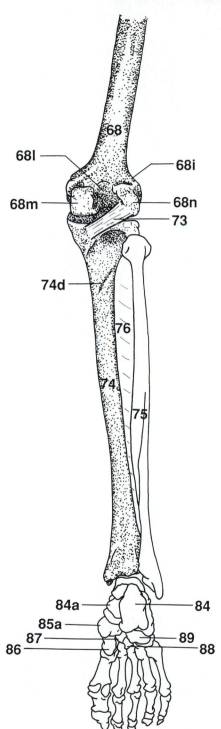

68. Femur
68i. Lateral supracondylar line (femur)
68l. Popliteal surface (femur)
68m. Medial condyle (femur)
68n. Lateral condyle (femur)
73. Oblique popliteal ligament
74. Tibia
74d. Soleal line (tibia)
75. Fibula
76. Interosseous membrane
84. Calcaneus
84a. Sustentaculum tali of calcaneus
85a. Tuberosity of navicular
86. Medial cuneiform
87. Intermediate cuneiform
88. Lateral cuneiform
89. Cuboid

RIGHT FOOT—PLANTAR VIEW

74e. Medial malleolus of tibia
79. Flexor retinaculum
80. Plantar aponeurosis
81. Plantar metatarsophalangeal ligaments
82. Transverse metatarsal ligaments
83. Talus
84a. Sustentaculum tali of calcaneus
84b. Tuberosity of calcaneus
84c. Medial border of calcaneus

84d. Lateral border of calcaneus
85a. Tuberosity of navicular
86. Medial cuneiform
87. Intermediate cuneiform
88. Lateral cuneiform
89. Cuboid
90. Metatarsal bones
91a. Proximal phalanges
91b. Middle phalanges
91c. Distal phalanges

CHAPTER TWO
MOVEMENTS OF THE BODY

Anatomical position—A subject in the anatomical position is standing erect with the head, eyes, and toes facing forward and the arms hanging straight at the sides with the palms of the hands facing forward.

Figure 2.1b
Coronal (frontal) planes—Pass vertically through the body from side to side. They divide the body from front to back.

Figure 2.1a
Median or midsagittal plane—Passes vertically through the body from anterior (front) to posterior (back). It divides the body into right and left sides. Other sagittal planes are parallel to this plane.

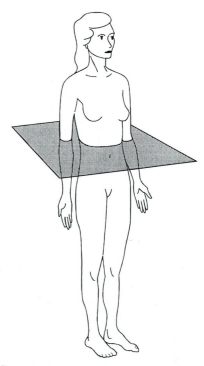

Figure 2.1c
Transverse planes (cross sections)—Pass horizontally through the body parallel to the ground.

Figure 2.2
Flexion—The left arm and forearm, and right thigh are drawn forward in sagittal planes. The right knee is also flexed.
Extension—The left thigh and knee are extended.
Hyperextension—The right arm is hyperextended at the shoulder.

Figure 2.3
Lateral flexion—The torso (or head) bends laterally in the coronal plane.

Figure 2.4
Abduction—The right arm is drawn laterally in the coronal plane.
Adduction—The left arm is returned from abduction to the anatomical position.

Figure 2.5
Medial rotation—The anterior of the arm (or thigh) is moved toward the median plane.
Lateral rotation—The anterior of the arm (or thigh) is moved away from the median plane.

MOVEMENTS OF THE SCAPULA

Figure 2.6a.
Elevation—The right
scapula of this figure is
drawn superiorly.

Figure 2.6b.
Depression—The right
scapula of this figure is
pushing the arm inferiorly.

Figure 2.6c
Protraction—The scapula pushes the arm forward in a
sagittal plane.

Figure 2.6d
Retraction—The scapula is pulled back from protraction
in a sagittal plane. Since the scapula slides around the
ribs toward the median plane it becomes adduction.

Figure 2.6e.
Rotation—For abduction of the arm to continue above the
height of the shoulder, the scapula must rotate on its axis
so that the glenoid fossa turns upward.

MOVEMENTS OF THE HAND AND FOREARM

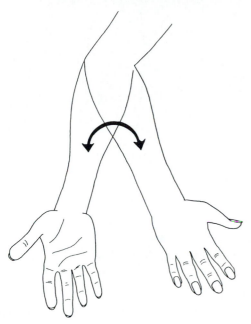

Figure 2.7
Pronation—The forearm is rotated away from the
anatomical position so that the palm turns medially then
posteriorly. If the forearm is flexed at the elbow then the
palm turns inferiorly.
Supination—The forearm is rotated so that the palm
turns anteriorly (or superiorly if the forearm is flexed).

Figure 2.8
Radial flexion (abduction)—The hand, at the wrist, is
drawn away from the body in a coronal plane.
Ulnar flexion (adduction)—The hand, at the wrist, is
drawn toward the body in a coronal plane.

Figure 2.9a
Abduction—The fingers are moved away from the midline
of the hand.

Figure 2.9b
Adduction—The fingers are moved toward the midline of
the hand.

Figure 2.9c
Opposition—The thumb is rotated so its anterior pad can
touch the anterior pads of the four fingers.

MOVEMENTS OF THE FOOT

Figure 2.11a
Eversion—The front of the foot moves laterally away from the midline (abduction) and the sole turns outward.

Figure 2.10
Dorsiflexion—The ankle flexes, moving the foot superiorly.
Plantar flexion—The ankle extends, moving the foot inferiorly.

Figure 2.11b
Inversion—The front of the foot moves medially toward the midline (adduction) and the sole turns inward.

CHAPTER THREE
MUSCLES OF THE FACE AND HEAD

EPICRANIUS

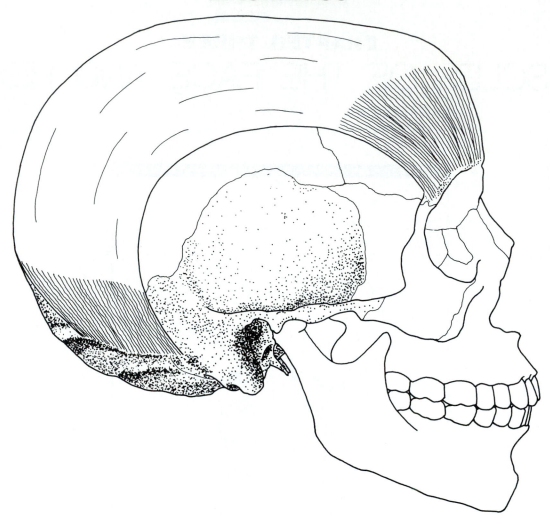

Skull—lateral view

Occipital belly   *(occipitalis)*

Origin   Lateral two-thirds of superior nuchal
                line of occipital bone, mastoid process
                of temporal bone

Insertion   Galea aponeurotica (an intermediate
                tendon leading to frontal belly)

Action   Draws back scalp, aids frontal belly to
                wrinkle forehead and raise eyebrows

Nerve   Posterior auricular branch of facial
                nerve

Frontal belly   *(frontalis)*

Origin   Galea aponeurotica

Insertion   Fascia of facial muscles and skin
                above nose and eyes

Action   Draws back scalp, wrinkles forehead,
                raises eyebrows

Nerve   Temporal branches of facial nerve

TEMPOROPARIETALIS

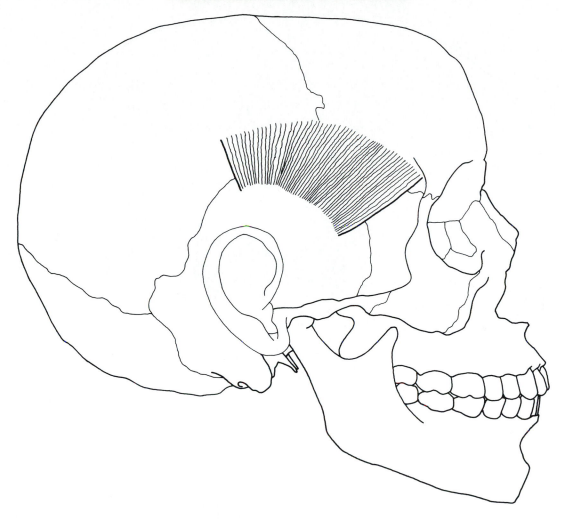

Skull—lateral view

Origin	Fascia over ear	**Action**	Raises ears, tightens scalp
Insertion	Lateral border of galea aponeurotica	**Nerve**	Temporal branch of facial nerve

AURICULARIS ANTERIOR, SUPERIOR, POSTERIOR

Skull—lateral view

Auricularis anterior

Origin	Fascia in temporal region
Insertion	Anterior to helix of ear
Action	Draws ear forward in some individuals, moves scalp*
Nerve	Temporal branch of facial nerve

Auricularis superior

Origin	Fascia in temporal region
Insertion	Superior part of ear
Action	Draws ear upward in some individuals, moves scalp*
Nerve	Temporal branch of facial nerve

Auricularis posterior

Origin	Mastoid area of temporal bone
Insertion	Posterior part of ear
Action	Draws ear upward in some individuals*
Nerve	Posterior auricular branch of facial nerve

*This muscle is nonfunctional in most people.

ORBICULARIS OCULI

ORBITAL AND PALPEBRAL PARTS   **LACRIMAL PART**

Skull—three-quarter anterior view

Orbital part

Origin	Frontal bone, maxilla (medial margin of orbit)
Insertion	Continues around orbit and returns to origin
Action	Strong closing of eye
Nerve	Temporal and zygomatic branches of facial nerve

Palpebral part   *(in eyelids)*

Origin	Medial palpebral ligament
Insertion	Lateral palpebral ligament into zygomatic bone
Action	Gentle closure of eyelids
Nerve	Temporal and zygomatic branches of facial nerve

Lacrimal part   *(behind medial palpebral ligament and lacrimal sac)*

Origin	Lacrimal bone
Insertion	Lateral palpebral raphe
Action	Draws lacrimal canals onto surface of eye
Nerve	Temporal and zygomatic branches of facial nerve

LEVATOR PALPEBRAE SUPERIORIS

Origin	Inferior surface of lesser wing of sphenoid
Insertion	Skin of upper eyelid
Action	Raises upper eyelid
Nerve	Oculomotor nerve

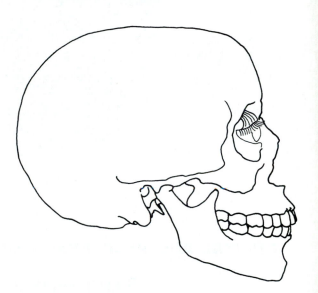

Skull—three-quarter anterior view   **Skull—lateral view**

CORRUGATOR SUPERCILII

Skull—anterior view

Origin Medial end of superciliary arch

Insertion Deep surface of skin under medial portion of eyebrows

Action Draws eyebrows downward and medially

Nerve Temporal branch of facial nerve

PROCERUS

Skull—anterior view

Origin	Fascia over nasal bone and lateral nasal cartilage	**Action**	Draws down medial part of eyebrows, wrinkles nose
Insertion	Skin between eyebrows	**Nerve**	Buccal branches of facial nerve

NASALIS

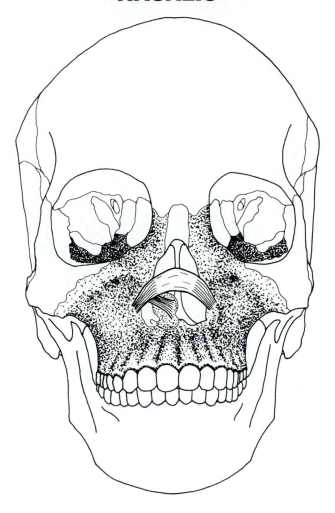

Skull—anterior view

Transverse part

Origin	Middle of maxilla
Insertion	Muscle of opposite side over bridge of nose

Alar part

Origin	Greater alar cartilage, skin on nose
Insertion	Skin at point of nose
Action	Both parts maintain opening of external nares during forceful inspiration
Nerve	Buccal branches of facial nerve

DEPRESSOR SEPTI

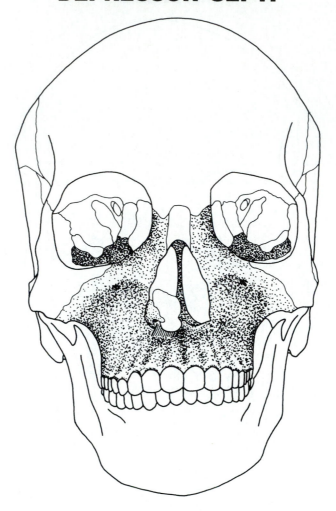

Skull—anterior view

Origin	Incisive fossa of maxilla	**Action**	Constricts nares
Insertion	Nasal septum and ala	**Nerve**	Buccal branches of facial nerve

ORBICULARIS ORIS

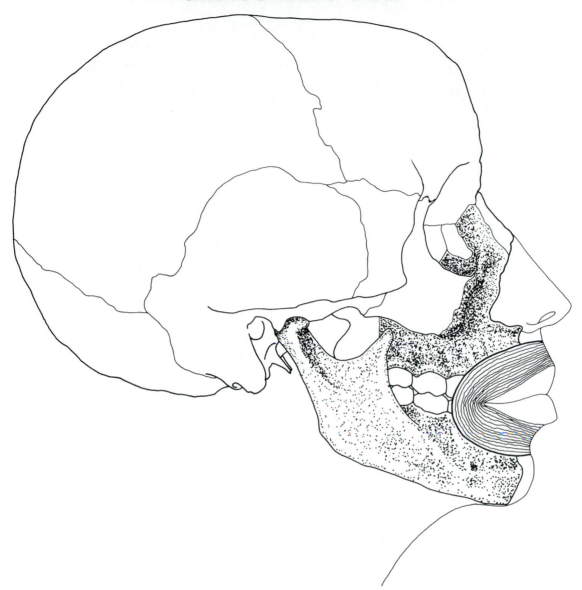

Skull—lateral view

Origin

Lateral band—alveolar border of maxilla
Medial band—septum of nose
Inferior portion—lateral to midline of mandible

Insertion

Becomes continuous with other muscles at angle of mouth

Action

Closure and protrusion of lips

Nerve

Buccal and mandibular branches of facial nerve

LEVATOR LABII SUPERIORIS

Skull—lateral view

Angular head

Origin	Frontal process of maxilla and zygomatic bone
Insertion	Greater alar cartilage and skin of nose, upper lip
Action	Elevates upper lip, dilates nares, forms nasolabial furrow
Nerve	Buccal branches of facial nerve

Infraorbital head

Origin	Lower margin of orbit
Insertion	Muscles of upper lip
Action	Elevates upper lip
Nerve	Buccal branches of facial nerve

LEVATOR ANGULI ORIS

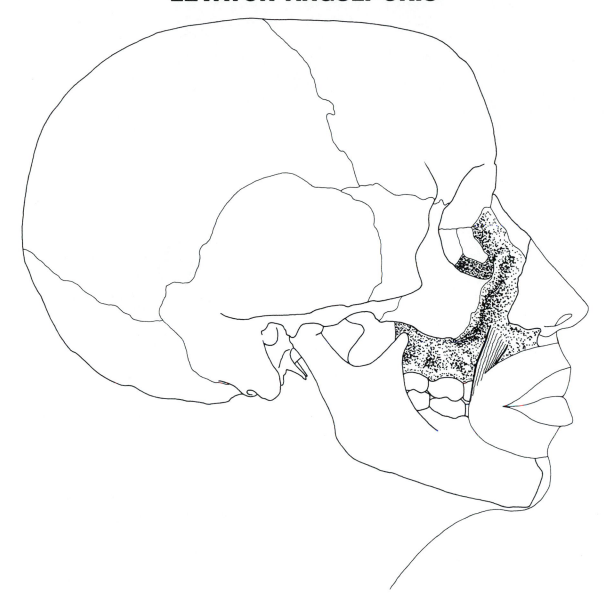

Skull—lateral view

Origin   Canine fossa of maxilla

Insertion   Angle of mouth

Action   Elevates the corner (angle) of the mouth

Nerve   Buccal branches of facial nerve

ZYGOMATICUS MAJOR

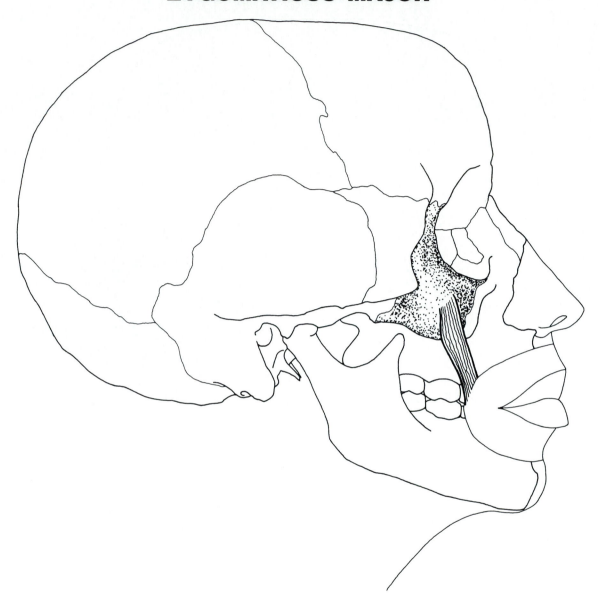

Skull—lateral view

Origin	Zygomatic bone	**Action**	Draws angle of mouth upward and backward (laughing)
Insertion	Angle of mouth	**Nerve**	Buccal branches of facial nerve

ZYGOMATICUS MINOR

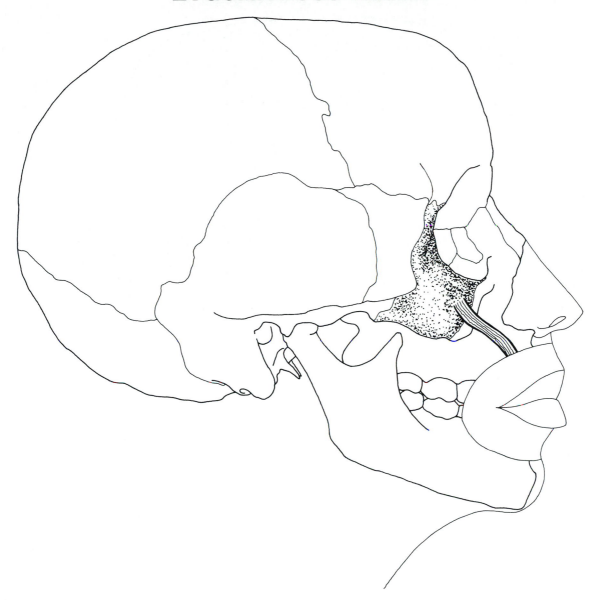

Skull—lateral view

Origin Zygomatic bone

Insertion Upper lip lateral to levator labii superioris

Action Forms nasolabial furrow

Nerve Buccal branches of facial nerve

RISORIUS

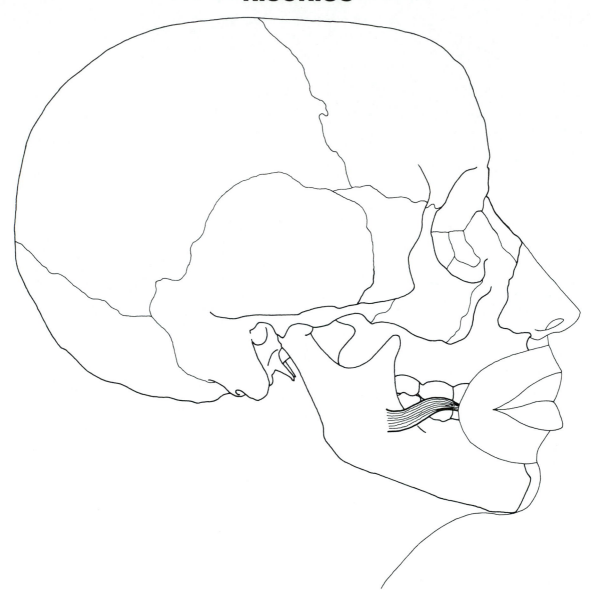

Skull—lateral view

Origin	Fascia over masseter	**Action**	Retracts angle of mouth, as in grinning
Insertion	Skin at angle of mouth	**Nerve**	Buccal branches of facial nerve

DEPRESSOR LABII INFERIORIS

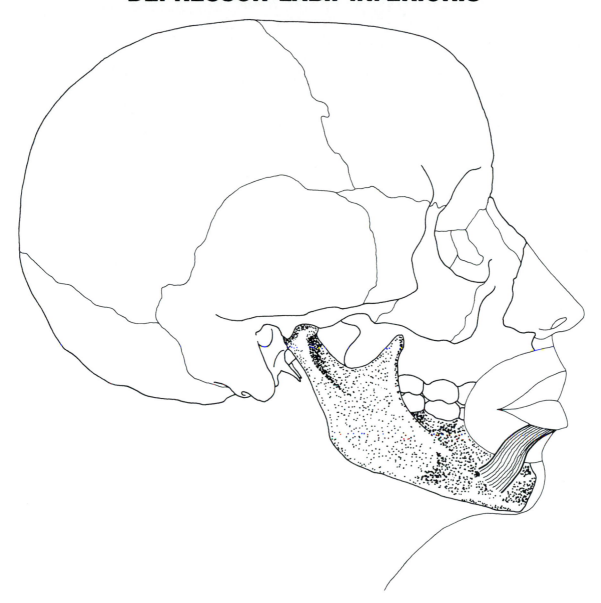

Skull—lateral view

Origin   Mandible, between symphysis and   **Action**   Draws lower lip downward and
               mental foramen   laterally

Insertion   Skin of lower lip   **Nerve**   Mandibular branch of facial nerve

DEPRESSOR ANGULI ORIS

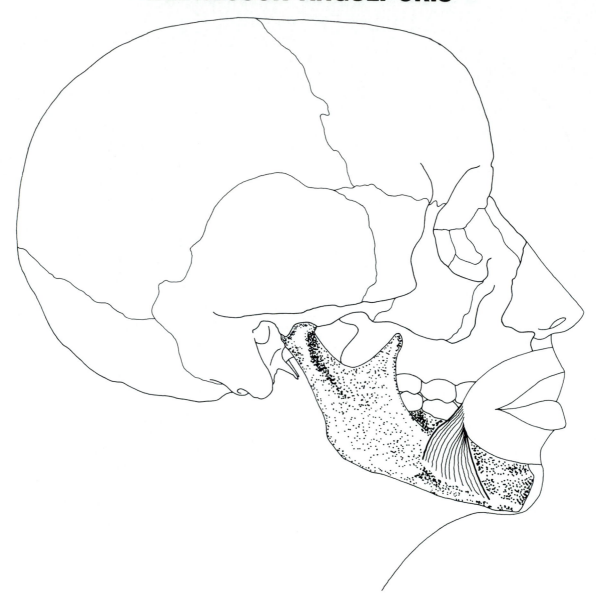

Skull—lateral view

Origin   Oblique line of the mandible
Insertion Angle of the mouth

Action   Depresses angle of mouth, as in frowning
Nerve   Mandibular branch of facial nerve

MENTALIS

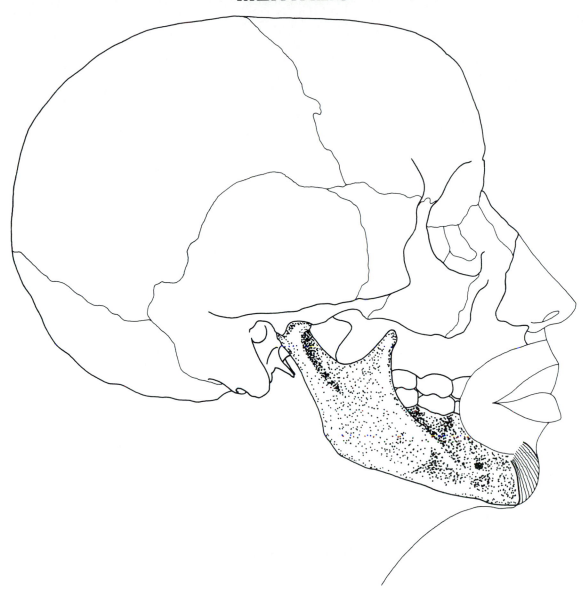

Skull—lateral view

Origin	Incisive fossa of mandible	**Action**	Raises and protrudes lower lip, wrinkles skin of chin
Insertion	Skin of chin	**Nerve**	Mandibular branch of facial nerve

BUCCINATOR

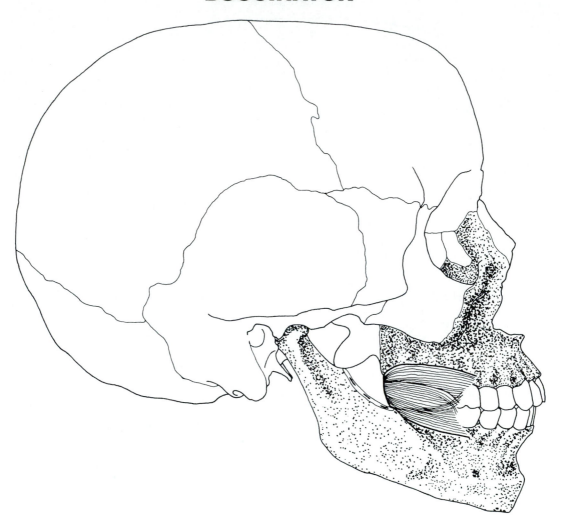

Skull—lateral view

Origin   Outer surface of alveolar processes of maxilla and mandible over molars and along pterygomandibular raphe

Insertion   Deep part of muscles of lips

Action   Compresses cheek

Nerve   Buccal branches of facial nerve

TEMPORALIS

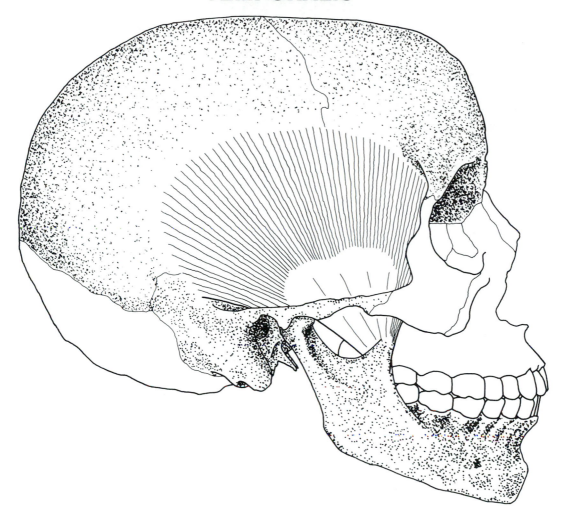

Skull—lateral view

Origin Temporal fossa including frontal, parietal, and temporal bones

Insertion Coronoid process and anterior border of ramus of mandible

Action Closes lower jaw, clenches teeth

Nerve Mandibular division of trigeminal nerve

MASSETER

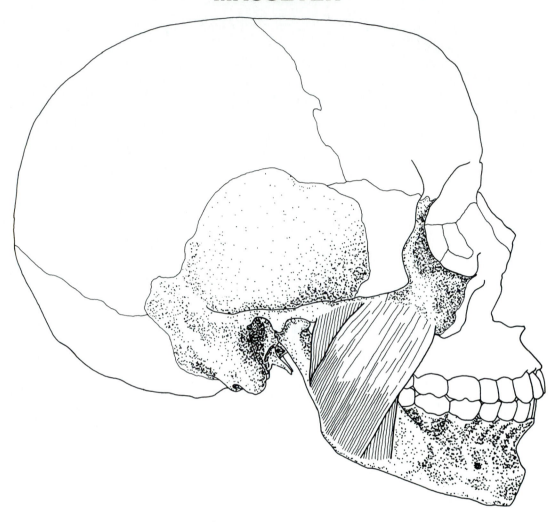

Skull—lateral view

Origin	Zygomatic process of maxilla, medial and inferior surfaces of zygomatic arch	**Action**	Closes lower jaw, clenches teeth
		Nerve	Mandibular division of trigeminal nerve
Insertion	Angle and ramus of mandible, lateral surface of coronoid process of mandible		

PTERYGOIDEUS MEDIALIS

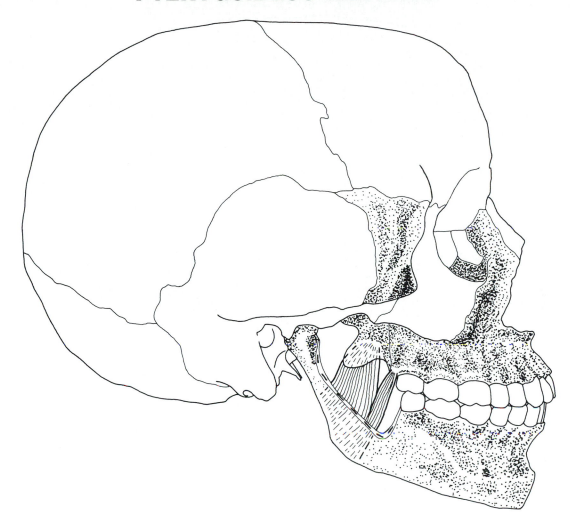

Skull—lateral view

(Part of mandible cut away)

Origin   Medial surface of lateral pterygoid plate
              of sphenoid bone, palatine bone, and
              tuberosity of maxilla

Insertion   Medial surface of ramus and angle of
              mandible

Action   Closes lower jaw, clenches teeth

Nerve   Mandibular division of trigeminal nerve

PTERYGOIDEUS LATERALIS

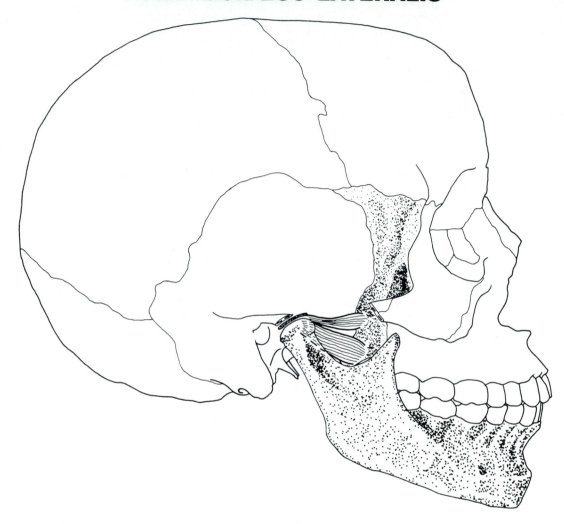

Skull—lateral view

Origin	Superior head—lateral surface of greater wing of sphenoid	**Action**	Opens jaws, protrudes mandible, moves mandible sidewards
	Inferior head—lateral surface of lateral pterygoid plate	**Nerve**	Mandibular division of trigeminal nerve
Insertion	Condyle of mandible, temporomandibular joint		

CHAPTER FOUR
MUSCLES OF THE NECK

STERNOCLEIDOMASTOIDEUS

Three-quarter frontal view

Origin	Sternal head—manubrium of sternum Clavicular head—medial part of clavicle	**Action**	One side—bends neck laterally, rotates head Both sides together—flexes neck, draws head ventrally and elevates chin, draws sternum superiorly in deep inspiration
Insertion	Mastoid process of temporal bone, lateral half of superior nuchal line of occipital bone		
		Nerve	Spinal part of accessory nerve (C2,C3)

PLATYSMA

Three-quarter frontal view

Origin   Subcutaneous fascia of upper one-fourth of chest

Insertion   Subcutaneous fascia and muscles of chin and jaw, mandible

Action   Depresses and draws lower lip laterally, draws up skin of chest

Nerve   Cervical branch of facial nerve

DIGASTRICUS

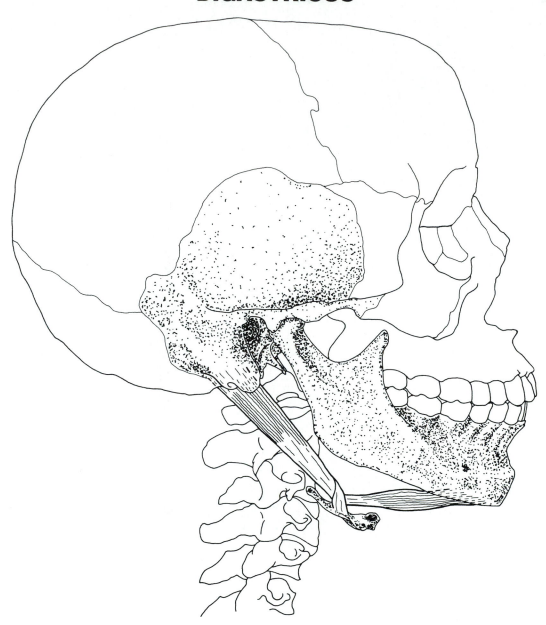

Lateral view

Origin	Posterior belly—mastoid notch of temporal bone	**Action**	Raises hyoid bone, assists in opening jaws, moves hyoid forward or backward
	Anterior belly—inner side of inferior border of mandible near symphysis	**Nerve**	Anterior belly—mandibular division of trigeminal
Insertion	Intermediate tendon attached to hyoid bone		Posterior belly—facial nerve

STYLOHYOIDEUS

Lateral view

Origin	Styloid process of temporal bone	**Action**	Draws hyoid bone backward, elevates tongue
Insertion	Hyoid bone	**Nerve**	Facial nerve

MYLOHYOIDEUS

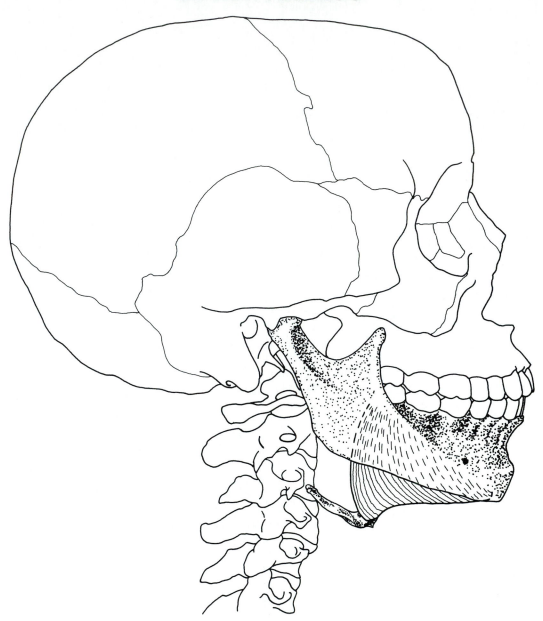

Lateral view

Origin Inside surface of mandible from symphysis to molars (mylohyoid line)

Insertion Hyoid bone

Action Elevates hyoid bone, raises floor of mouth and tongue

Nerve Mandibular division of trigeminal nerve

GENIOHYOIDEUS

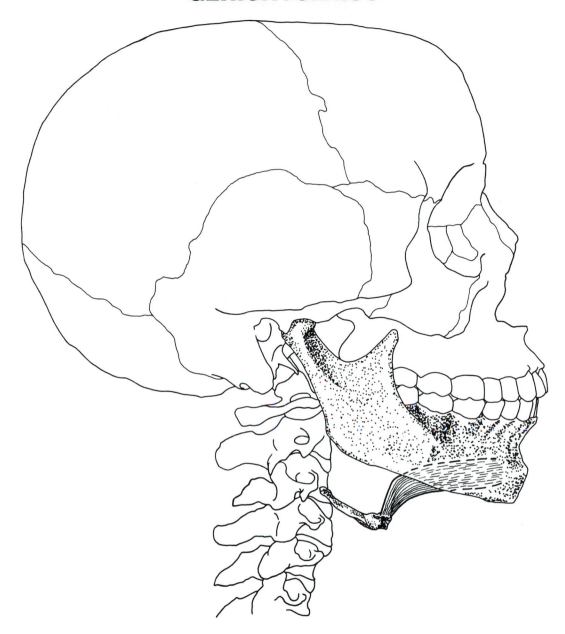

Lateral view

Origin   Inferior mental spine on interior medial   **Action**   Protrudes hyoid bone and tongue
                surface of mandible   **Nerve**   Branch of C1 through hypoglossal
Insertion   Body of hyoid bone   nerve

STERNOHYOIDEUS

Frontal view

Origin	Medial end of clavicle, manubrium of sternum
Insertion	Body of hyoid bone
Action	Depresses hyoid bone
Nerve	Ansa cervicalis (C1–C3)

Lateral view

STERNOTHYROIDEUS

Frontal view

Origin	Dorsal surface of manubrium of sternum
Insertion	Lamina of thyroid cartilage
Action	Depresses thyroid cartilage
Nerve	Ansa cervicalis (C1–C3)

Lateral view

THYROHYOIDEUS

Lateral view

Origin	Lamina of thyroid cartilage	**Action**	Depresses hyoid or raises thyroid
Insertion	Greater cornu of hyoid bone	**Nerve**	C1 through hypoglossal nerve

OMOHYOIDEUS

Lateral view

Origin	Superior border of scapula	**Action**	Depresses hyoid bone
Insertion	Inferior belly—bound to clavicle by central tendon Superior belly—continues to body of hyoid bone	**Nerve**	Ansa cervicalis (C2,C3)

LONGUS COLLI

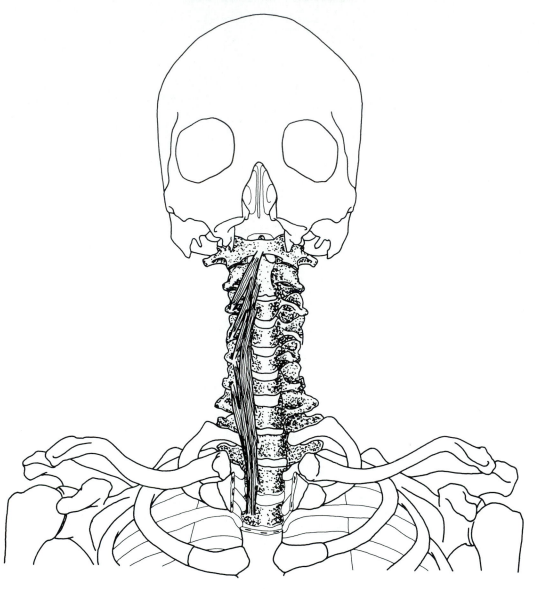

Frontal view

(Mandible and part of maxilla removed)

Superior oblique part

Origin	Transverse processes of third, fourth, and fifth cervical vertebrae
Insertion	Anterior arch of atlas

Inferior oblique part

Origin	Anterior surface of bodies of first two or three thoracic vertebrae
Insertion	Transverse processes of fifth and sixth cervical vertebrae

Vertical part

Origin	Anterior surfaces of bodies of upper three thoracic and lower three cervical vertebrae
Insertion	Anterior surfaces of the second, third, and fourth cervical vertebrae
Action	All three parts flex cervical vertebrae
Nerve	C2–C7

LONGUS CAPITIS

Frontal view

(Mandible and part of maxilla removed)

Origin Transverse processes of third through sixth cervical vertebrae

Insertion Occipital bone anterior to foramen magnum

Action Flexes head

Nerve C1–C3

RECTUS CAPITIS ANTERIOR

Frontal view

(Mandible and part of maxilla removed)

Origin   Anterior base of transverse process of atlas

Insertion   Occipital bone anterior to foramen magnum

Action   Flexes head

Nerve   C2,C3

RECTUS CAPITIS LATERALIS

Frontal view

(Mandible and part of maxilla removed)

Origin   Transverse process of atlas   **Action**   Bends head laterally

Insertion   Jugular process of occipital bone   **Nerve**   C2,C3

SCALENUS ANTERIOR

Three-quarter frontal view
(Mandible and part of maxilla removed)

Origin	Transverse processes of third through sixth cervical vertebrae	**Action**	Raises first rib (inspiration), flexes and rotates neck
Insertion	Inner border of first rib (scalene tubercle)	**Nerve**	Ventral rami of cervical nerves

SCALENUS MEDIUS

Three-quarter frontal view

(Mandible and part of maxilla removed)

Origin	Transverse processes of lower six cervical vertebrae (C2–C7)	**Action**	Raises first rib (inspiration), flexes and rotates neck
Insertion	Upper surface of first rib	**Nerve**	Ventral rami of cervical nerves

SCALENUS POSTERIOR

Three-quarter frontal view

(Mandible and part of maxilla removed)

Origin	Transverse processes of lower two or three cervical vertebrae (C5–C7)	**Action**	Raises second rib (inspiration), flexes and rotates neck
Insertion	Outer surface of second rib	**Nerve**	Ventral rami of lower cervical nerves

RECTUS CAPITIS POSTERIOR MAJOR

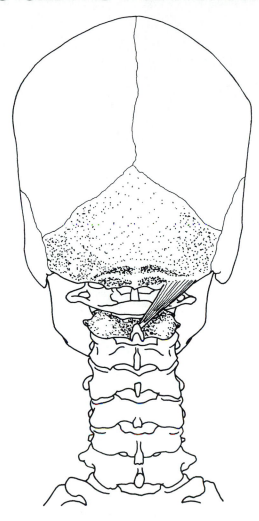

Posterior skull and cervical vertebrae

Origin Spinous process of axis

Insertion Lateral portion of inferior nuchal line of occipital bone

Action Extends and rotates head

Nerve Suboccipital nerve

RECTUS CAPITIS POSTERIOR MINOR

Posterior skull and cervical vertebrae

Origin	Posterior arch of atlas	**Action**	Extends head
Insertion	Medial portion of inferior nuchal line of occipital bone	**Nerve**	Suboccipital nerve

OBLIQUUS CAPITIS INFERIOR

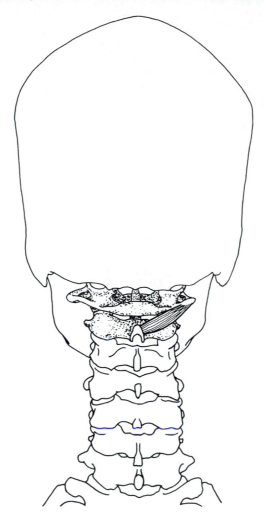

Posterior skull and cervical vertebrae

Origin	Spinous process of axis	**Action**	Rotates atlas
Insertion	Transverse process of atlas	**Nerve**	Suboccipital nerve

OBLIQUUS CAPITIS SUPERIOR

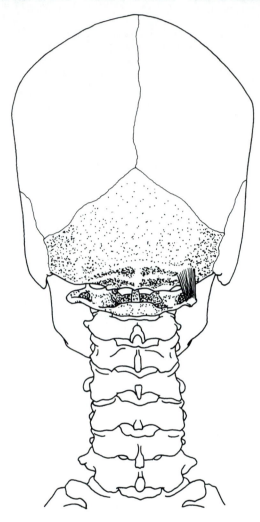

Posterior skull and cervical vertebrae

Origin	Transverse process of atlas	**Action**	Extends and bends head laterally
Insertion	Occipital bone between inferior and superior nuchal lines	**Nerve**	Suboccipital nerve

CHAPTER FIVE
MUSCLES OF THE TRUNK

SPLENIUS CAPITIS

Posterior skull, neck, and back

Origin   Lower part of ligamentum nuchae, spinous processes of seventh cervical vertebra (C7) and upper three or four thoracic vertebrae (T1–T4)

Insertion   Mastoid process of temporal bone and lateral part of superior nuchal line

Action   Extends and rotates the head

Nerve   Lateral branches of dorsal primary divisions of middle and lower cervical nerves

SPLENIUS CERVICIS*

Posterior skull, neck, and back

Origin   Spinous processes of third through sixth thoracic vertebrae (T3–T6)

Insertion   Transverse processes of upper two or three cervical vertebrae (C1–C3)

Action   Extends and rotates the head

Nerve   Lateral branches of dorsal primary divisions of middle and lower cervical nerves

ERECTOR SPINAE*

ILIOCOSTALIS LUMBORUM

Origin	Medial and lateral sacral crests and medial part of iliac crests
Insertion	Angles of lower six ribs
Action	Extension, lateral flexion of vertebral column, rotates ribs for forceful inspiration
Nerve	Dorsal primary divisions of spinal nerves

ILIOCOSTALIS THORACIS

Origin	Angles of lower six ribs medial to iliocostalis lumborum
Insertion	Angles of upper six ribs and transverse process of seventh cervical vertebra
Action	Extension, lateral flexion of vertebral column, rotates ribs for forceful inspiration
Nerve	Dorsal primary divisions of spinal nerves

ILIOCOSTALIS CERVICIS

Origin	Angles of third through sixth ribs
Insertion	Transverse processes of fourth, fifth, and sixth cervical vertebrae
Action	Extension, lateral flexion of vertebral column
Nerve	Dorsal primary divisions of spinal nerves

*The erector spinae (sacrospinalis) is a complex of three sets of muscles: iliocostalis, longissimus, and spinalis. The origin of this group is the medial and lateral sacral crests, the medial part of iliac crests, and the spinous processes and supraspinal ligament of lumbar and eleventh and twelfth thoracic vertebrae.

Trunk—dorsal view

ERECTOR SPINAE

LONGISSIMUS THORACIS

Origin   Medial and lateral sacral crests, spinous processes and supraspinal ligament of lumbar and eleventh and twelfth thoracic vertebrae, and medial part of iliac crests

Insertion   Transverse processes of all thoracic vertebrae, between tubercles and angles of lower nine or ten ribs

Action   Extension, lateral flexion of vertebral column, rotates ribs for forceful inspiration

Nerve   Dorsal primary divisions of spinal nerves

LONGISSIMUS CERVICIS

Origin   Transverse processes of upper four or five thoracic vertebrae (T1–T5)

Insertion   Transverse processes of second through sixth cervical vertebrae

Action   Extension, lateral flexion of vertebral column

Nerve   Dorsal primary divisions of spinal nerves

LONGISSIMUS CAPITIS

Origin   Transverse processes of upper five thoracic vertebrae (T1–T5), articular processes of lower three cervical vertebrae (C5–C7)

Insertion   Posterior part of mastoid process of temporal bone

Action   Extends and rotates head

Nerve   Dorsal primary divisions of middle and lower cervical nerves

Trunk—dorsal view

ERECTOR SPINAE

SPINALIS THORACIS

Origin	Spinous processes of lower two thoracic (T11, T12) and upper two lumbar (L1, L2) vertebrae
Insertion	Spinous processes of upper thoracic vertebrae (T1–T8)
Action	Extends vertebral column
Nerve	Dorsal primary divisions of spinal nerves

SPINALIS CERVICIS

Origin	Ligamentum nuchae, spinous process of seventh cervical vertebra
Insertion	Spinous process of axis
Action	Extends vertebral column
Nerve	Dorsal primary divisions of spinal nerves

SPINALIS CAPITIS

(Medial part of semispinalis capitis)

Trunk—dorsal view

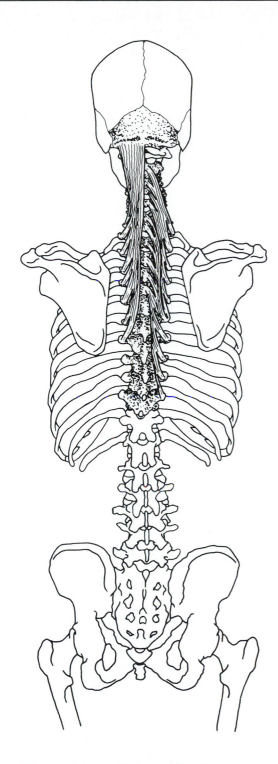

Trunk—dorsal view

TRANSVERSOSPINALIS*

SEMISPINALIS THORACIS

Origin	Transverse processes of the sixth through tenth thoracic vertebrae (T6–T10)
Insertion	Spinous processes of the lower two cervical (C6, C7) and upper four thoracic (T1–T4) vertebrae
Action	Extends and rotates vertebral column
Nerve	Dorsal primary divisions of spinal nerves

SEMISPINALIS CERVICIS

Origin	Transverse processes of upper five or six thoracic vertebrae (T1–T6)
Insertion	Spinous processes of second to fifth cervical vertebrae (C2–C5)
Action	Extends and rotates vertebral column
Nerve	Dorsal primary divisions of spinal nerves

SEMISPINALIS CAPITIS

(Medial part is spinalis capitis)

Origin	Transverse processes of lower four cervical (C4–C7) and upper six or seven thoracic (T1–T7) vertebrae
Insertion	Between superior and inferior nuchal lines of occipital bone
Action	Extends and rotates head
Nerve	Dorsal primary divisions of spinal nerves

*The transversospinalis is made up of groups of small muscles generally extending upward from transverse processes to spinous processes of higher vertebrae. They are deep to erector spinae. They include semispinalis, multifidi, and rotatores.

MULTIFIDIS*

Origin	Sacral region—along sacral foramina up to posterior superior iliac spine Lumbar region—mamillary processes of vertebrae Thoracic region—transverse processes Cervical region—articular processes of lower four vertebrae (C4–C7)
Insertion	Spinous process two to four vertebrae superior to origin
Action	Extend and rotate vertebral column
Nerve	Dorsal primary division of spinal nerves

*Part of transversospinalis

Trunk—dorsal view

ROTATORES*

Origin	Transverse process of each vertebra
Insertion	Base of spinous process of next vertebra above
Action	Extend and rotate vertebral column
Nerve	Dorsal primary division of spinal nerves

*Part of transversospinalis

Trunk—dorsal view

INTERSPINALES*

(Paired on either side of interspinal ligament)

Origin	Cervical region—spinous processes of third to seventh cervical vertebrae (C3–C7) Thoracic region—spinous processes of second to twelfth thoracic vertebrae (T2–T12) Lumbar region—spinous processes of second to fifth lumbar vertebrae (L2–L5)
Insertion	Spinous process of next vertebra superior to origin
Action	Extend vertebral column
Nerve	Dorsal primary division of spinal nerves

Trunk—dorsal view

Trunk—dorsal view

INTERTRANSVERSARII*
Cervical region

INTERTRANSVERSARII ANTERIORES

Origin	Anterior tubercle of transverse processes of vertebrae from first thoracic to axis
Insertion	Anterior tubercle of next superior vertebra
Action	Lateral flexion of vertebral column
Nerve	Ventral primary division of spinal nerves

INTERTRANSVERSARII POSTERIORES

Origin	Posterior tubercle of transverse processes of vertebrae from first thoracic to axis
Insertion	Posterior tubercle of next superior vertebra

Thoracic region

Origin	Transverse processes of first lumbar to eleventh thoracic vertebrae
Insertion	Transverse processes of next superior vertebra

Lumbar region

INTERTRANSVERSARII LATERALES

Origin	Transverse processes of lumbar vertebrae
Insertion	Transverse process of next superior vertebra
Action	Lateral flexion of vertebral column
Nerve	Ventral primary division of spinal nerves

INTERTRANSVERSARII MEDIALES

Origin	Mamillary process of each lumbar vertebra
Insertion	Accessory process of the next superior lumbar vertebra
Action	Lateral flexion of vertebral column
Nerve	Dorsal primary division of spinal nerves

INTERCOSTALES EXTERNI

Trunk—anterior view

Origin	Lower margin of upper eleven ribs	**Action**	Draw ventral part of ribs upward, increasing the volume of the thoracic cavity for inspiration
Insertion	Superior border of rib below (each muscle fiber runs obliquely and inserts toward the costal cartilage)	**Nerve**	Intercostal nerves

INTERCOSTALES INTERNI

Trunk—anterior view

Origin From the cartilages to the angles of the upper eleven ribs

Insertion Superior border of the rib below (each muscle fiber runs obliquely and inserts away from the costal cartilage)

Action Draw ventral part of ribs downward, decreasing the volume of the thoracic cavity for expiration

Nerve Intercostal nerves

SUBCOSTALES

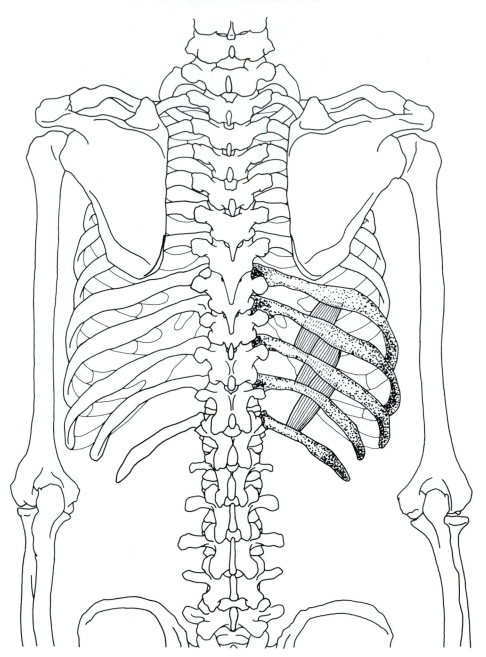

Trunk—dorsal view

Origin	Inner surface of each rib near its angle	**Action**	Draw ventral part of ribs downward, decreasing the volume of the thoracic cavity for forceful expiration
Insertion	Medially on the inner surface of second or third rib below		
		Nerve	Intercostal nerves

TRANSVERSUS THORACIS

Trunk—anterior view

Origin Inner surface of lower portion of sternum and adjacent costal cartilages

Insertion Inner surfaces of costal cartilages of the second through sixth ribs

Action Draws ventral part of ribs downward, decreasing the volume of the thoracic cavity for forceful expiration

Nerve Intercostal nerves

LEVATORES COSTARUM

Trunk—dorsal view

Origin   Transverse processes of the seventh cervical and the upper eleven thoracic vertebrae

Insertion   Laterally to outer surface of next lower rib (lower muscles may cross over one rib)

Action   Raises ribs; extends, laterally flexes, and rotates vertebral column

Nerve   Intercostal nerves

SERRATUS POSTERIOR SUPERIOR

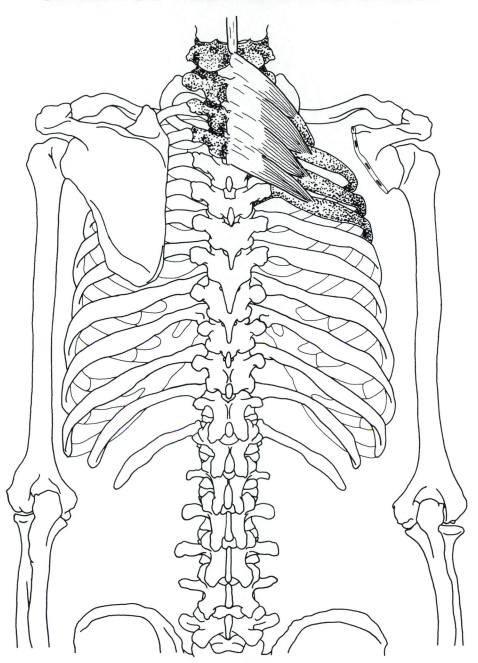

Trunk—dorsal view

Origin   Ligamentum nuchae, spinous processes of seventh cervical and first few thoracic vertebrae

Insertion   Upper borders of the second through fifth ribs lateral to their angles

Action   Raises ribs in inspiration

Nerve   T1–T4

SERRATUS POSTERIOR INFERIOR

Trunk—dorsal view

Origin	Spinous processes of the lower two thoracic and the upper two or three lumbar vertebrae	**Action**	Pulls ribs down, resisting pull of diaphragm
Insertion	Lower borders of bottom four ribs	**Nerve**	T9–T12

DIAPHRAGM

Trunk—anterior view

(Lower costal cartilages removed)

Origin

Sternal part—inner part of xiphoid process
Costal part—inner surfaces of lower six ribs and their cartilages
Lumbar part—upper two or three lumbar vertebrae and lateral and medial lumbocostal arches

Insertion Fibers converge and meet on a central tendon

Action Draws central tendon inferiorly

Nerve Phrenic nerve (C3–C5)

Note: This muscle is unique because it inserts upon itself. Its action is to change the volume of the thoracic and abdominal cavities.

OBLIQUUS EXTERNUS ABDOMINIS

Trunk—lateral view

Origin	Lower eight ribs	**Nerve**	Eighth to twelfth intercostal, iliohypogastric, ilioinguinal nerves
Insertion	Anterior part of iliac crest, abdominal aponeurosis to linea alba	**Relationships**	Most superficial of the three lateral abdominal muscles
Action	Compresses abdominal contents, laterally flexes and rotates vertebral column		

OBLIQUUS INTERNUS ABDOMINIS

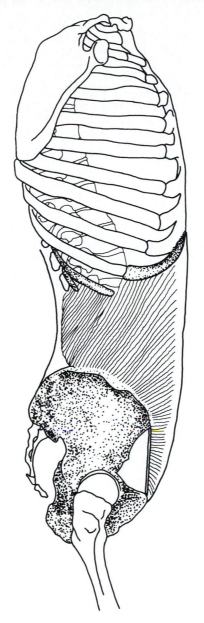

Trunk—lateral view

Origin	Lateral half of inguinal ligament, iliac crest, thoracolumbar fascia	**Nerve**	Eighth to twelfth intercostal, iliohypogastric, ilioinguinal nerves
Insertion	Cartilage of bottom three or four ribs, abdominal aponeurosis to linea alba	**Relationships**	Middle layer of the three lateral abdominal muscles
Action	Compresses abdominal contents, laterally flexes and rotates vertebral column		

CREMASTER

Trunk—anterior view

Origin	Inguinal ligament	**Action**	Pulls testes toward body
Insertion	Pubic tubercle, crest of pubis, sheath of rectus abdominis	**Nerve**	Genital branch of genitofemoral nerve

Note: The cremaster regulates the temperature of the testes, which is important for spermatogenesis.

TRANSVERSUS ABDOMINIS

Trunk—lateral view

Origin Lateral part of inguinal ligament, iliac crest, thoracolumbar fascia, cartilage of lower six ribs

Insertion Abdominal aponeurosis to linea alba

Action Compresses abdomen

Nerve Seventh to twelfth intercostal, iliohypogastric, ilioinguinal nerves

Relationships Deepest of the three lateral abdominal muscles

RECTUS ABDOMINIS*

Origin	Crest of pubis, pubic symphysis
Insertion	Cartilage of fifth, sixth, and seventh ribs, xiphoid process
Action	Flexes vertebral column, compresses abdomen
Nerve	Seventh through twelfth intercostal nerves

*Tendinous bands divide each rectus into three or four bellies. Each rectus is sheathed in aponeurotic fibers from the lateral abdominal muscles. These fibers meet centrally to form the linea alba.

Note: The pyramidalis is a small, unimportant muscle that extends from the ventral surface of the pubis to the lower part of the linea alba. It is frequently absent.

Trunk—anterior view

ABDOMINAL MUSCLES

Trunk—anterior and cross-sectional views

1. Obliquus externus abdominis
2. Obliquus internus abdominis
3. Transversus abdominis
4. Rectus abdominis
5. Linea alba

Note: The aponeuroses (tendons) of the three lateral abdominal muscles join to form the fascial sheath surrounding the rectus abdominis.

QUADRATUS LUMBORUM

Lower trunk—anterior view

Origin	Iliolumbar ligament, iliac crest	**Action**	Laterally flexes vertebral column, fixes ribs for forced expiration
Insertion	Twelfth rib, transverse processes of upper four lumbar vertebrae	**Nerve**	T12, L1

Note: Fixation of ribs may provide a stable attachment of the diaphragm for voice control in singers.

CHAPTER SIX
MUSCLES OF THE SHOULDER AND ARM

PECTORALIS MAJOR

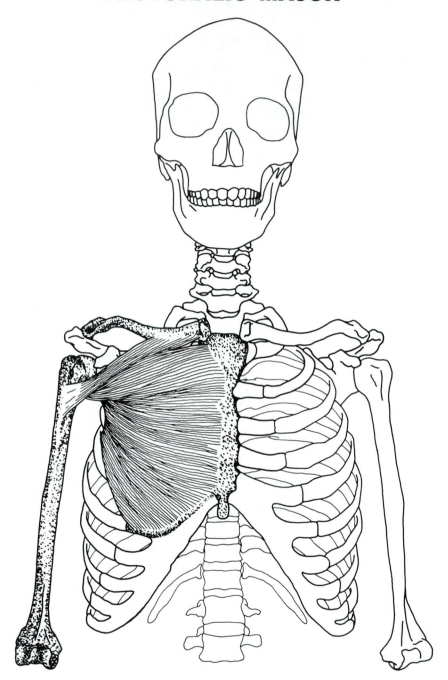

Anterior view

Origin	Clavicular part—medial half of the clavicle	**Action**	Both parts adduct, medially rotate arm; clavicular part flexes arm from full extension; sternocostal part extends the flexed arm
	Sternocostal part—sternum, upper six costal cartilages, aponeurosis of external oblique		
Insertion	Lateral lip of intertubercular (bicipital) groove of humerus, crest below greater tubercle of the humerus	**Nerve**	Medial and lateral pectoral nerves (C5–C8, T1)

PECTORALIS MINOR

Anterior view

Origin	External surfaces of the third, fourth, and fifth ribs	**Nerve**	Medial pectoral nerve (C8, T1)
Insertion	Coracoid process of the scapula	**Relationships**	Deep to pectoralis major
Action	Draws scapula forward and downward, raises ribs in forced inspiration		

SUBCLAVIUS

Anterior view

Origin	Junction of the first rib with its costal cartilage	**Action**	Depresses clavicle, draws shoulder forward and downward, steadies clavicle during movements of shoulder girdle
Insertion	Groove on the inferior (lower) surface of the clavicle	**Nerve**	C5, C6

CORACOBRACHIALIS

Anterior view

Origin	Tip (apex) of the coracoid process of scapula	**Nerve**	Musculocutaneous nerve (C6, C7)
Insertion	Middle third of the medial surface and border of the humerus	**Relationships**	Deep to short head of biceps
Action	Weakly adducts arm (flexion unsubstantiated)		

BICEPS BRACHII

Anterior view

Origin	Long head—supraglenoid tubercle of scapula Short head—coracoid process of scapula	**Action**	Supinates forearm, flexes forearm, weakly flexes arm at shoulder
		Nerve	Musculocutaneous nerve (C5, C6)
Insertion	Tuberosity of radius, bicipital aponeurosis into deep fascia on medial part of forearm	**Relationships**	Long head passes through intertubercular (bicipital) groove, then inside glenohumeral joint capsule

BRACHIALIS

Anterior view

Origin   Anterior of lower half of humerus   **Action**   Flexes forearm

Insertion   Coronoid process of ulna, tuberosity   **Nerve**   Musculocutaneous nerve (C5, C6)
of ulna

Relationships   Deep to biceps brachii

MUSCLES OF THE ANTERIOR CHEST AND ARM

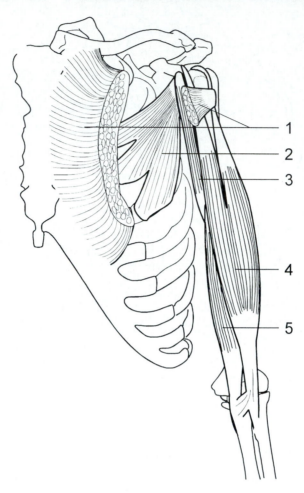

Shoulder—anterior view

1. Pectoralis major (cut)   **4.** Biceps brachii
2. Pectoralis minor   **5.** Brachialis
3. Coracobrachialis

TRAPEZIUS

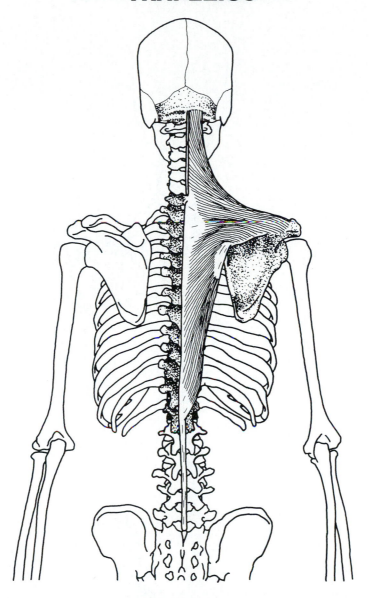

Posterior view

Origin	Medial third of superior nuchal line, external occipital protuberance, ligamentum nuchae, spinous processes and supraspinous ligaments of seventh cervical and all thoracic vertebrae	**Action**	Upper part elevates scapula, middle part retracts (adducts) scapula, lower part depresses scapula, upper and lower parts together rotate scapula (important in elevating arm)
Insertion	Upper part—lateral third of clavicle Middle part—acromion and crest of spine of scapula Lower part—medial portion of crest of spine of scapula (tubercle)	**Nerve** **Relationships**	Accessory (11th cranial), C3, C4 Most superficial muscle of back

LATISSIMUS DORSI

Posterior view

Origin   Spinous processes of the lower six
                 thoracic vertebrae, lumbar vertebrae,
                 sacral vertebrae, supraspinal
                 ligament, and posterior part of the
                 iliac crest through the lumbar
                 (thoracolumbar) fascia, lower three or
                 four ribs, inferior angle of the scapula

Insertion   Floor (bottom) of the bicipital groove
                 of humerus

Action   Extends, adducts, and medially
                 rotates the arm, draws the shoulder
                 downward and backward, keeps
                 inferior angle of scapula against the
                 chest wall, accessory muscle of
                 respiration

Nerve   Thoracodorsal nerve (C6–C8)

Note: This muscle is used for the crawl stroke in swimming.

LEVATOR SCAPULAE

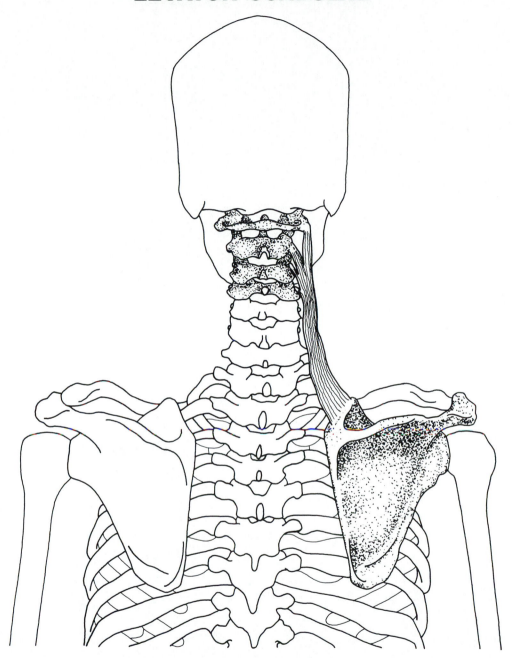

Posterior view

Origin Posterior tubercles of the transverse processes of the first four cervical vertebrae

Insertion Vertebral (medial) border of the scapula at and above the spine

Action Elevates medial border of scapula, rotates scapula to lower the lateral angle, acts with trapezius and rhomboids to pull scapula medially and upward, bends neck laterally

Nerve Dorsal scapular nerve (C5)

RHOMBOIDEUS MAJOR

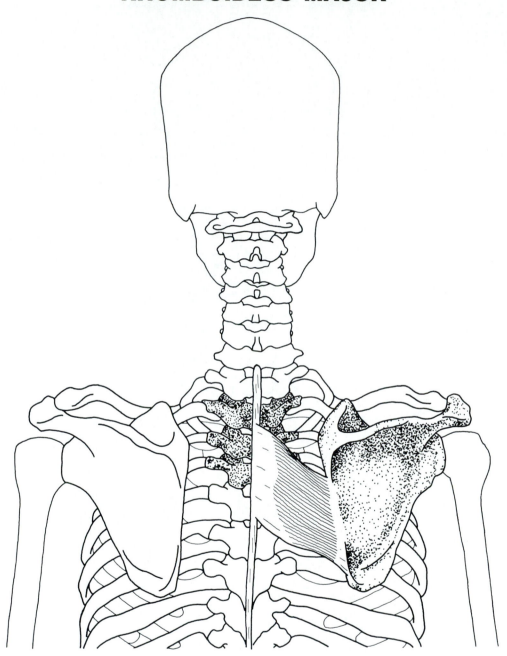

Posterior view

Origin	Spines of the second to fifth thoracic vertebrae, supraspinous ligament	**Action**	Retracts and fixes scapula, elevates the medial border of the scapula, rotates the scapula to depress the lateral angle (assists in adduction of arm)
Insertion	Medial border of the scapula below the spine		
		Nerve	Dorsal scapular nerve (C5)

RHOMBOIDEUS MINOR

Posterior view

Origin	Spines of the seventh cervical and first thoracic vertebrae, lower part of the ligamentum nuchae	**Action**	Retracts and fixes scapula, elevates the medial border of the scapula, rotates the scapula to depress the lateral angle (assists in adduction of arm)
Insertion	Medial border of the scapula at the root of the spine	**Nerve**	Dorsal scapular nerve (C5)

Lateral view

SERRATUS ANTERIOR

Origin Outer surfaces and superior borders of first eight or nine ribs, and fascia covering first intercostal space

Insertion Anterior surface (costal surface) of the medial border of the scapula

Action Rotates scapula for abduction and flexion of arm, protracts scapula

Nerve Long thoracic nerve (C5–C7)

Relationships Serratus anterior and rhomboids both insert on the medial border of scapula; they are antagonists causing protraction and retraction

DELTOIDEUS

Origin	Anterior portion—anterior border and superior surface of the lateral third of the clavicle
	Middle portion—lateral border of the acromion process
	Posterior portion—lower border of the crest of the spine of the scapula
Insertion	Deltoid tuberosity, on the middle of the lateral surface of the shaft of the humerus
Action	Anterior portion—flexes and medially rotates arm
	Middle portion—abducts arm
	Posterior portion—extends and laterally rotates arm
Nerve	Axillary nerve (C5, C6)

Lateral view

Lateral view

SUPRASPINATUS
(Rotator cuff*)

Origin	Supraspinous fossa of scapula
Insertion	Upper part of the greater tuberosity of the humerus, capsule of the shoulder joint
Action	Aids deltoid in abduction of arm, draws humerus toward glenoid fossa preventing deltoid from forcing humerus up against acromion, weakly flexes arm
Nerve	Suprascapular nerve (C5)

*Supraspinatus, infraspinatus, teres minor, and subscapularis together are called the rotator cuff. They prevent the larger muscles from dislocating the humerus during their actions.

INFRASPINATUS
(Rotator cuff)

Origin	Infraspinous fossa of the scapula
Insertion	Middle facet of the greater tuberosity of the humerus, capsule of the shoulder joint
Action	Draws humerus toward glenoid fossa thus resisting posterior dislocation of arm as in crawling; laterally rotates; abducts arm
Nerve	Suprascapular nerve (C5, C6)

Lateral view

TERES MINOR
(Rotator cuff)

Origin	Upper two-thirds of the dorsal surface of the axillary border of the scapula
Insertion	The capsule of the shoulder joint, the lower facet of the greater tuberosity of the humerus
Action	Laterally rotates arm, weakly adducts arm, draws humerus toward glenoid fossa
Nerve	Axillary nerve (C5)

Lateral view

SUBSCAPULARIS
(Rotator cuff)

Anterior view
(Upper ribs cut away)

Origin	Subscapular fossa on the anterior surface of scapula	**Action**	Medially rotates arm, stabilizes glenohumeral joint
Insertion	Lesser tuberosity of the humerus, ventral part of the capsule of the shoulder joint	**Nerve**	Upper and lower subscapular nerves (C5, C6)

TERES MAJOR

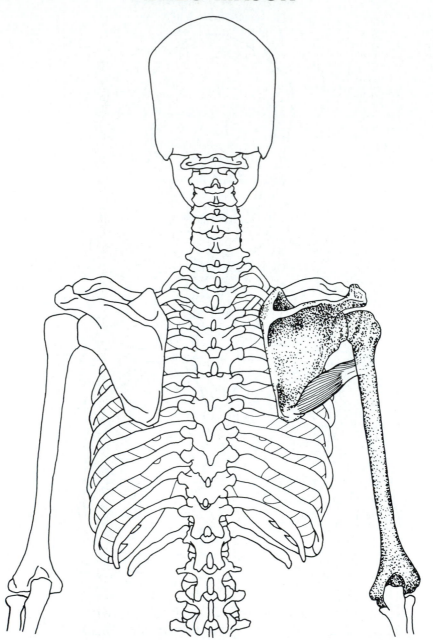

Posterior view

Origin	Lower third of the posterior surface of the lateral border of the scapula, near the inferior angle	**Action**	Medially rotates arm, adducts arm, extends arm
Insertion	Medial lip of the bicipital groove of the humerus	**Nerve**	Lower subscapular nerve (C5, C6)

TRICEPS BRACHII

Posterior view

Origin	Long head—infraglenoid tubercle of the scapula	**Insertion**	Posterior part of olecranon process of the ulna
	Lateral head—upper half of the posterior surface of the shaft of the humerus	**Action**	Extends forearm, long head aids in adduction if arm is abducted
	Medial head—posterior surface of the lower half of the shaft of the humerus	**Nerve**	Radial nerve (C7, C8)

Note: The radial nerve comes from the axilla (armpit) and passes along the humerus between the medial and lateral heads. Because of its position it is the most commonly injured peripheral nerve.

ANCONEUS

Posterior view of arm

Origin	Posterior part of lateral epicondyle of the humerus	**Action**	Extends forearm (assists triceps)
Insertion	Lateral surface of the olecranon process and posterior surface of ulna	**Nerve**	Radial nerve (C7, C8)

POSTERIOR BACK, SHOULDER, AND ARM MUSCLES

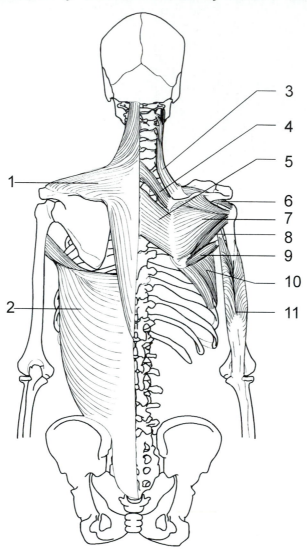

Trunk—dorsal view

Superficial layer
1. Trapezius
2. Latissimus dorsi
Deep layer
3. Levator scapulae
4. Rhomboideus minor
5. Rhomboideus major

6. Supraspinatus (rotator cuff)
7. Infraspinatus (rotator cuff)
8. Teres minor (rotator cuff)
9. Teres major
10. Serratus anterior
Posterior arm
11. Triceps brachii

CHAPTER SEVEN
MUSCLES OF THE FOREARM AND HAND

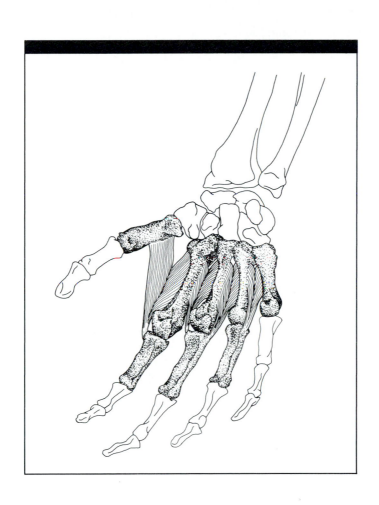

PRONATOR TERES
(Superficial group)

Origin	Humeral head—medial supracondylar ridge and medial epicondyle of the humerus
	Ulnar head—medial border of the coronoid process of the ulna
Insertion	Middle of lateral surface of the radius (pronator tuberosity)
Action	Pronates and flexes forearm
Nerve	Median nerve (C6, C7)

Forearm—anterior view

FLEXOR CARPI RADIALIS
(Superficial group)

Origin	Medial epicondyle of the humerus through the common tendon
Insertion	Front of the bases of the second and third metacarpal bones
Action	Flexes hand, synergist in abduction with extensor carpi radialis longus and brevis
Nerve	Median nerve (C6, C7)

Forearm—anterior view

PALMARIS LONGUS

(Superficial group)

Origin	Medial epicondyle of the humerus through the common tendon
Insertion	Front (central part) of the flexor retinaculum and apex of the palmar aponeurosis
Action	Flexes the hand
Nerve	Median nerve (C6, C7)

Note: This muscle is absent in about 14% of limbs.

Reference:
Agur, Amr: *Grant's Atlas of Anatomy,* 9th ed. Williams & Wilkins, Baltimore, 1991.

Forearm—anterior view

FLEXOR CARPI ULNARIS
(Superficial group)

Origin	Humeral head—medial epicondyle of the humerus through the common tendon
	Ulnar head—medial margin of olecranon process of ulna, dorsal border of shaft of the ulna
Insertion	Pisiform bone, hook of the hamate, and base of the fifth metacarpal bone
Action	Flexes hand, synergist in adduction of hand with extensor carpi ulnaris
Nerve	Ulnar nerve (C8, T1)

Forearm—anterior view

MUSCLES OF THE WRIST

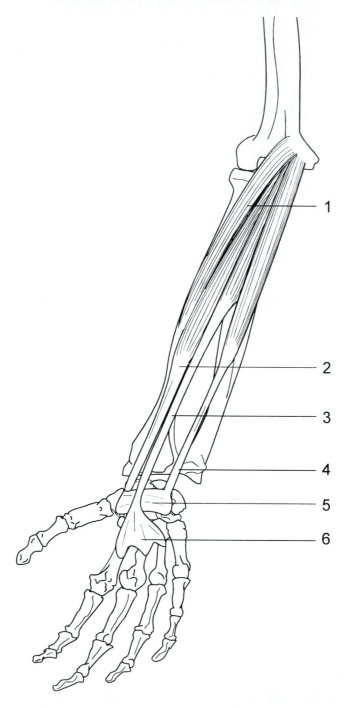

1
2
3
4
5
6

Forearm—anterior view

1. Pronator teres
2. Flexor carpi radialis
3. Palmaris longus
4. Flexor carpi ulnaris
5. Flexor retinaculum
6. Palmar aponeurosis

FLEXOR DIGITORUM SUPERFICIALIS

Origin   Humeroulnar head—medial epicondyle of the humerus through common tendon,* medial margin of the coronoid process of ulna
Radial head—anterior surface of shaft of radius

Insertion   Four tendons divide into two slips each, slips insert into the sides (margins of the anterior surfaces) of the middle phalanges of four fingers

Action   Flexes the middle phalanges of the fingers

Nerve   Median nerve (C7, C8, T1)

Relationships   Deep to superficial flexors

*See superficial flexors

Forearm—anterior view

FLEXOR DIGITORUM PROFUNDUS

Origin   Upper three-fourths of anterior and
                      medial surfaces of shaft of ulna and
                      medial side of the coronoid process,
                      interosseous membrane

Insertion   Front of base of distal phalanges of
                      fingers

Action   Flexes distal phalanges

Nerve   Ulnar nerve supplies the medial half of
                      the muscle (going to the little and ring
                      fingers) (C8, T1)
                      Anterior interosseous branch of median
                      nerve supplies lateral half (going to
                      index and middle fingers) (C8, T1)

Relationships   Deep to flexor digitorum superficialis

Note: Both flexor digitorum muscles and the median nerve pass under
the flexor retinaculum (page 10) in the wrist. When irritated, the
synovial sheaths of these muscles can compress the median nerve
causing the sensory and motor deficits known as carpal tunnel
syndrome.

Forearm—anterior view

FLEXOR POLLICIS LONGUS

Origin Middle of anterior surface of shaft of radius, interosseous membrane, medial epicondyle of humerus, and often coronoid process of ulna

Insertion Palmar aspect of base of the distal phalanx of thumb

Action Flexes the thumb

Nerve Anterior interosseous branch of median nerve (C8, T1)

Forearm—anterior view

FLEXORS OF THE FINGERS

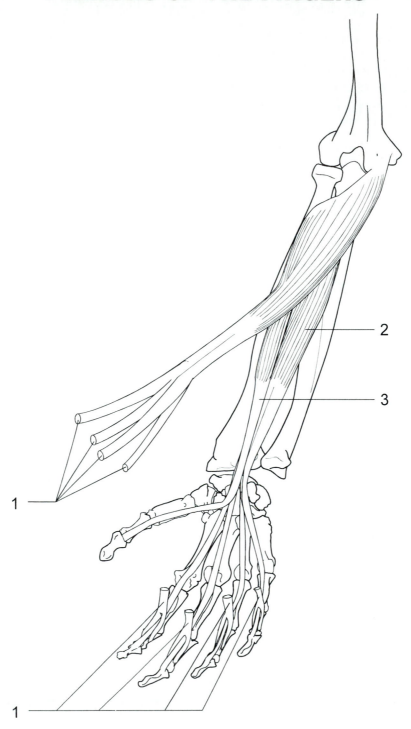

Forearm—anterior view

1. Flexor digitorum superficialis (cut)
2. Flexor digitorum profundus
3. Flexor pollicis longus

PRONATOR QUADRATUS

Origin	Anterior surface of distal part of shaft of ulna
Insertion	Lower portion of anterior surface of shaft of radius, distal part of lateral border of radius
Action	Pronates forearm and hand
Nerve	Anterior interosseous branch of median nerve (C8, T1)
Relationships	Deepest forearm muscle

Forearm—anterior view

BRACHIORADIALIS

Forearm—dorsal view

Origin Upper two-thirds of lateral supracondylar ridge of humerus

Insertion Base of styloid process and lateral surface of radius

Action Flexes forearm

Nerve Radial nerve (C5, C6)

EXTENSOR CARPI RADIALIS LONGUS

Forearm—dorsal view

Origin	Lower third of lateral supracondylar ridge of humerus	**Action**	Extends hand, synergist in abduction of hand with flexor carpi radialis
Insertion	Posterior surface of the base of the second metacarpal bone	**Nerve**	Radial nerve (C6, C7)

EXTENSOR CARPI RADIALIS BREVIS

Forearm—dorsal view

Origin	Lateral epicondyle of humerus	**Action**	Extends hand, synergist in abduction of hand with flexor carpi radialis
Insertion	Dorsal surface of third metacarpal bone	**Nerve**	Radial nerve (C6, C7)

EXTENSOR DIGITORUM COMMUNIS

Forearm and hand—dorsal view

Origin	Common tendon attached to lateral epicondyle of humerus	**Nerve**	Deep branch of radial nerve (C6–C8)
Insertion	Lateral and dorsal surfaces of all the phalanges of the four fingers	**Relationships**	Tends to hyperextend the metacarpophalangeal joint causing "claw hand"; its action is balanced by the lumbricales and interossei
Action	Extends the fingers and wrist		

EXTENSOR DIGITI MINIMI

Forearm and hand—dorsal view

Origin   Common tendon attached to lateral
             epicondyle of humerus

Insertion   Dorsum of first phalanx of little finger

Action   Extends little finger

Nerve   Radial nerve (C6–C8)

EXTENSOR CARPI ULNARIS

Forearm and hand—dorsal view

Origin	Common tendon attached to lateral epicondyle of humerus	**Action**	Extends hand, synergist in adduction of hand with flexor carpi ulnaris
Insertion	Posterior surface of base of fifth metacarpal bone	**Nerve**	Radial nerve (C6–C8)

SUPINATOR

Origin	Lateral epicondyle of humerus, lateral ligament (radial collateral) of elbow, annular ligament of superior radioulnar joint, supinator crest of ulna
Insertion	Dorsal and lateral surfaces of upper third of radius
Action	Supinates forearm
Nerve	Radial nerve (C6)

Forearm and hand—anterior view

ABDUCTOR POLLICIS LONGUS

Forearm and hand—dorsal view

Origin	Posterior (dorsal) surface of shaft of radius, ulna, interosseous membrane	**Action**	Abducts, laterally rotates, and extends thumb; abducts wrist
Insertion	Posterior surface of base of first metacarpal bone	**Nerve**	Radial nerve (C6, C7)

EXTENSOR POLLICIS BREVIS

Forearm and hand—dorsal view

Origin	Posterior surface of radius, adjacent part of interosseous membrane	**Action**	Extends thumb, abducts hand
Insertion	Base of proximal phalanx of thumb	**Nerve**	Radial nerve (C6, C7)

EXTENSOR POLLICIS LONGUS

Forearm and hand—dorsal view

Origin   Middle third of dorsal surface of ulna,   **Action**   Extends thumb
                    interosseous membrane   **Nerve**   Radial nerve (C6–C8)
Insertion   Base of distal phalanx of thumb

EXTENSORS OF THE THUMB

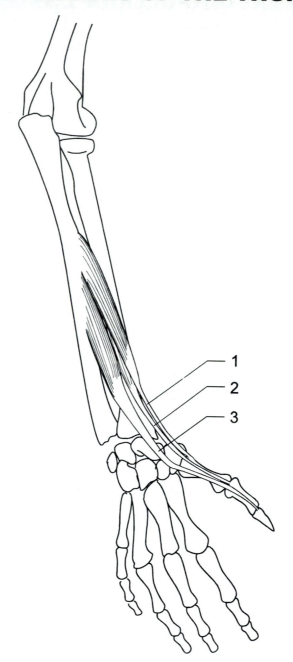

1
2
3

Forearm—posterior view

1. Abductor pollicis longus
2. Extensor pollicis brevis
3. Extensor pollicis longus

EXTENSOR INDICIS

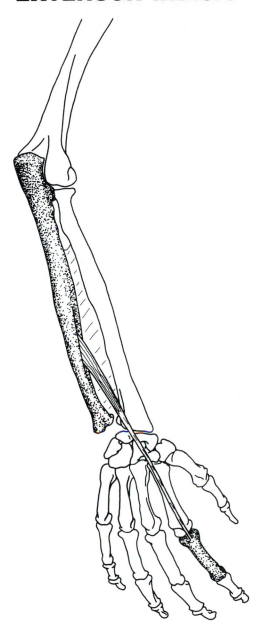

Forearm and hand—dorsal view

Origin	Posterior surface of ulna and adjacent part of interosseous membrane	**Action**	Extends index finger
Insertion	Extensor expansion on back of proximal phalanx of index finger	**Nerve**	Radial nerve (C6–C8)

PALMARIS BREVIS

Hand—palmar view

Origin	Flexor retinaculum, palmar aponeurosis	**Action**	Corrugates skin of palm
Insertion	Skin of the palm	**Nerve**	Ulnar nerve (C8)

ABDUCTOR POLLICIS BREVIS

(Thenar eminence)

Hand—palmar view

Origin	Tubercle of scaphoid, tubercle of trapezium, flexor retinaculum	**Action**	Abducts thumb and moves it anteriorly, acts together with other muscles of thenar eminence to oppose thumb to other fingers
Insertion	Base of proximal phalanx of thumb	**Nerve**	Median (C6, C7)

Note: The abductor pollicis brevis, flexor pollicis brevis, and opponens pollicis form the thenar eminence at the base of the thumb.

FLEXOR POLLICIS BREVIS
(Thenar eminence)

Hand—palmar view

Origin	Flexor retinaculum and trapezium, and first metacarpal bone	**Action**	Flexes metacarpophalangeal joint of thumb, assists in abduction and rotation of thumb, acts together with other muscles of thenar eminence to oppose thumb to other fingers
Insertion	Base of proximal phalanx of thumb		
		Nerve	Lateral portion—median nerve (C6, C7) Medial portion—ulnar nerve (C8, T1)

OPPONENS POLLICIS
(Thenar eminence)

Hand—palmar view

Origin	Flexor retinaculum, tubercle of trapezium	**Action**	Rotates thumb into opposition with fingers, acts together with other muscles of thenar eminence to oppose thumb to other fingers
Insertion	Lateral border of first metacarpal bone		
		Nerve	Median nerve (C6, C7)

ADDUCTOR POLLICIS

Hand—palmar view

Origin

Oblique head—anterior surfaces of second and third metacarpals, capitate, trapezoid
Transverse head—anterior surface of third metacarpal bone

Insertion

Medial side of base of proximal phalanx of the thumb

Action

Adducts thumb

Nerve

Ulnar nerve (C8, T1)

ABDUCTOR DIGITI MINIMI
(Hypothenar eminence)

Hand—palmar view

Origin	Pisiform bone, tendon of flexor carpi ulnaris	**Action**	Abducts little finger
Insertion	Medial side of base of proximal phalanx of little finger	**Nerve**	Ulnar nerve (C8, T1)

Note: The hypothenar eminence is less prominent than the thenar eminence and the fifth finger obviously cannot oppose the other digits.

FLEXOR DIGITI MINIMI BREVIS
(Hypothenar eminence)

Hand—palmar view

Origin	Anterior surface of flexor retinaculum, hook of hamate	**Action**	Flexes little finger at metacarpophalangeal joint
Insertion	Medial side of base of proximal phalanx of little finger	**Nerve**	Ulnar nerve (C8, T1)

OPPONENS DIGITI MINIMI
(Hypothenar eminence)

Hand—palmar view

Origin   Anterior surface of flexor retinaculum, hook of hamate

Insertion Whole length of medial border of fifth metacarpal bone

Action   Rotates fifth metacarpal bone, draws fifth metacarpal bone forward, assists flexor digiti minimi brevis in flexing carpometacarpal joint of little finger

Nerve   Ulnar nerve (C8, T1)

LUMBRICALES*
(Four muscles)

Hand—palmar view

Origin	Tendons of flexor digitorum profundus in palm	**Nerve**	Lateral lumbricals (first and second)—median nerve (C6, C7)
Insertion	Lateral side of corresponding tendon of extensor digitorum on fingers		Medial lumbricals (third and fourth)—ulnar nerve (C8)
Action	Extend fingers at interphalangeal joints, weakly flex fingers at metacarpophalangeal joints	**Relationships**	Assist extensor digitorum communis in extending fingers without hyperextension at the metacarpophalangeal joints

*Associated with the tendons of flexor digitorum profundus

PALMAR INTEROSSEI

Hand—palmar view

Origin

First—medial side of base of first metacarpal bone

Second, third, and fourth—anterior surfaces of second, fourth, and fifth metacarpal bones

Insertion

First—medial side of base of proximal phalanx of thumb

Second—medial side of base of proximal phalanx of index finger

Third and fourth—lateral side of proximal phalanges of ring finger and little finger

Action

Adduct fingers toward center of third finger at metacarpophalangeal joints, assist in flexion of fingers at metacarpophalangeal joints

Nerve

Ulnar nerve (C8, T1)

Note: The palmar interosseus of the thumb, called the palmar interosseus of Henle, is usually absent.

DORSAL INTEROSSEI

Hand—palmar view

Origin   By two heads from adjacent sides of
first and second, second and third,
third and fourth, and fourth and fifth
metacarpal bones

Third—medial side of base of
proximal phalanx of middle finger
Fourth—medial side of base of
proximal phalanx of ring finger

Insertion   First—lateral side of base of proximal
phalanx of index finger
Second—lateral side of base of
proximal phalanx of middle finger

Action   Abduct fingers away from center of
third finger at metacarpophalangeal
joints, assist in flexion of fingers at
metacarpophalangeal joints

Nerve   Ulnar nerve (C8, T1)

CHAPTER EIGHT
MUSCLES OF THE HIP AND THIGH

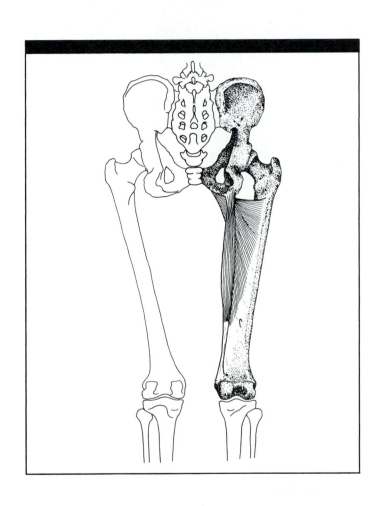

PSOAS MAJOR
(Part of iliopsoas)

Lumbar region, hip, and thigh—anterior view

Origin   Bases of transverse processes of all lumbar vertebrae, bodies of twelfth thoracic and all lumbar vertebrae, intervertebral disks above each lumbar vertebra

Insertion   Lesser trochanter of femur

Action   Flexes thigh at hip joint, flexes vertebral column

Nerve   Branches from lumbar plexus (L2, L3) and sometimes L1 or L4

Note: Some upper fibers insert onto the hip bone from the arcuate line to the iliopectineal eminence to form the *psoas minor*. This muscle has little function and is frequently absent.

ILIACUS

(Part of iliopsoas)

Lumbar region, hip, and thigh—anterior view

Origin   Upper two-thirds of iliac fossa, ala of
             sacrum and adjacent ligaments,
             anterior inferior iliac spine

Insertion   Onto tendon of psoas major, which
             continues into lesser trochanter of
             femur (together the two muscles form
             the iliopsoas)

Action   Flexes thigh at hip joint

Nerve   Femoral nerve (L2, L3)

Note: The iliacus brings swinging leg forward in walking or running.

PIRIFORMIS

Hip and thigh—anterior view

Origin　Internal surface of sacrum, sacrotuberous ligament

Insertion　Upper border of greater trochanter

Action　Laterally rotates thigh at hip joint, abducts thigh

Nerve　Anterior rami of first and second sacral nerves

Note: The common peroneal part of the sciatic nerve may emerge through the belly of the piriformis instead of below its inferior border along with the tibial part.

OBTURATOR INTERNUS

Hip—posterior view

Origin	Pelvic surface of obturator membrane and surrounding bones (ilium, ischium, pubis)	**Action**	Laterally rotates thigh at hip joint
Insertion	Common tendon with superior and inferior gemelli to medial surface of greater trochanter	**Nerve**	Nerve from sacral plexus (L5, S1–S3)

GEMELLUS SUPERIOR

Hip—posterior view

Origin   Spine of ischium

Insertion   With tendon of obturator internus into upper border of greater trochanter

Action   Laterally rotates thigh at hip joint

Nerve   Branch of nerve to obturator internus from sacral plexus

GEMELLUS INFERIOR

Hip—posterior view

Origin   Upper margin of ischial tuberosity

Insertion   With tendon of obturator internus into upper border of greater trochanter

Action   Laterally rotates thigh at hip joint

Nerve   Branch of nerve to quadratus femoris from sacral plexus

OBTURATOR EXTERNUS

Hip and thigh—anterior view

Origin　　Outer surface of superior and inferior rami of pubis and ramus of ischium surrounding obturator foramen

Insertion　　Trochanteric fossa of femur

Action　　Laterally rotates thigh

Nerve　　Obturator nerve (L3, L4)

Note: Part of this muscle can be seen posteriorly by separating the gemellus inferior and quadratus femoris. It is deep within this cleft.

QUADRATUS FEMORIS

Hip and thigh—posterior view

Origin	Lateral border of ischial tuberosity	**Action**	Laterally rotates thigh at hip joint
Insertion	Below intertrochanteric crest (quadrate line)	**Nerve**	Branch from sacral plexus (L5, S1)

GLUTEUS MAXIMUS

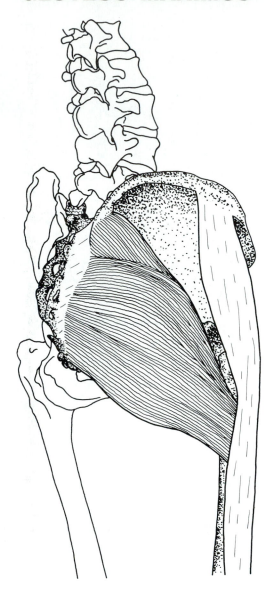

Hip and thigh—lateral view

Origin Outer surface of ilium behind posterior gluteal line, adjacent posterior surface of sacrum and coccyx, sacrotuberous ligament, aponeurosis of erector spinae (sacrospinalis)

Insertion Iliotibial tract of fascia lata, gluteal tuberosity of femur

Action Upper part—abducts, laterally rotates thigh
Lower part—extends, laterally rotates thigh, extends trunk

Nerve Inferior gluteal nerve (L5, S1, S2)

Note: This is not a postural muscle; it is not used in walking but only in forceful extension as in running, climbing, or rising from a seated position.

GLUTEUS MEDIUS

Hip and thigh—lateral view

Origin	Outer surface of ilium inferior to iliac crest	**Nerve**	Superior gluteal nerve (L4, L5, S1)
Insertion	Lateral surface of greater trochanter		
Action	Abducts femur at hip joint and rotates thigh medially		

Note: In locomotion, this muscle (along with the gluteus minimus) prevents the pelvis from dropping (adduction of thigh) toward the opposite swinging leg.

GLUTEUS MINIMUS

Hip and thigh—lateral view

Origin   Outer surface of ilium between middle   **Action**   Abducts femur at hip joint and rotates
              (anterior) and inferior gluteal lines   thigh medially

Insertion   Anterior surface of greater trochanter   **Nerve**   Superior gluteal nerve (L4, L5, S1)

Note: See note on gluteus medius.

MUSCLES OF THE HIP

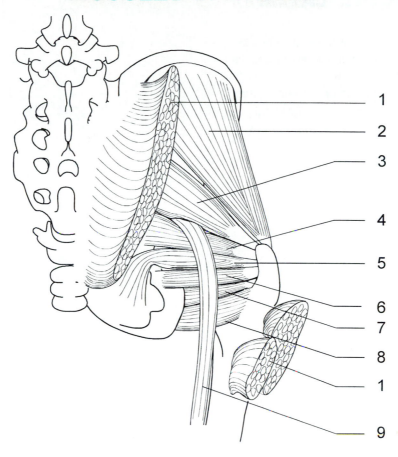

Hip—posterior view

1. Gluteus maximus (cut)
2. Gluteus medius
3. Piriformis
4. Gemellus superior
5. Obturator internus
6. Gemellus inferior
7. Obturator externus
8. Quadratus femoris
9. Sciatic nerve

Note: Gemellus inferior and quadratus femoris have been shown separated to expose the deeply placed obturator externus.

TENSOR FASCIAE LATAE

Origin	Outer edge of iliac crest between anterior superior iliac spine and iliac tubercle
Insertion	Iliotibial tract on upper part of thigh
Action	Flexes and medially rotates thigh
Nerve	Superior gluteal nerve (L4, L5, S1)

Hip and thigh—lateral view

SARTORIUS

Origin	Anterior superior iliac spine and area immediately below it
Insertion	Upper part of medial surface of shaft of tibia
Action	Flexes, abducts, and laterally rotates thigh at hip joint, flexes and slightly medially rotates leg at knee joint after flexion
Nerve	Femoral nerve (L2, L3)
Relationship	Insertions of sartorius, gracilis, and semitendinosus fuse on the medial tibia; these tendons, called the pes anserinus (goose foot), give medial support to the knee

Note: This muscle is used to bring swinging leg forward in walking and running.

Hip, thigh, and leg—anterior view

RECTUS FEMORIS
(One of quadriceps femoris)

Origin	Anterior head—anterior inferior iliac spine Posterior head—ilium above acetabulum
Insertion	Patella, then by patellar ligament to tuberosity of the tibia
Action	Extends leg at knee joint, flexes thigh at hip joint
Nerve	Femoral nerve (L2–L4)

Note: This muscle is used when thigh flexion and leg extension are needed together such as in kicking a football. In walking, the quadriceps prevent the knee from flexing during heel strike and early support phase.

Hip, thigh, and leg—anterior view

VASTUS LATERALIS

(One of quadriceps femoris)

Origin	Intertrochanteric line, inferior border of greater trochanter, gluteal tuberosity, lateral lip of linea aspera of femur
Insertion	Lateral margin of patella, then by patellar ligament to tuberosity of tibia
Action	Extends leg at knee joint
Nerve	Femoral nerve (L2–L4)

Hip, thigh, and leg—anterior view

VASTUS MEDIALIS
(One of quadriceps femoris)

Origin   Intertrochanteric line, medial lip of
              linea aspera of femur, medial
              intermuscular septum, medial
              supracondylar line

Insertion   Medial border of the patella, then by
              patellar ligament into tibial tuberosity,
              medial condyle of tibia

Action   Extends leg at knee joint

Nerve   Femoral nerve (L2–L4)

Hip, thigh, and leg—anterior view

VASTUS INTERMEDIUS
(One of quadriceps femoris)

Origin	Anterior and lateral surfaces of upper two-thirds of femur, lateral intermuscular septum, linea aspera, lateral supracondylar line
Insertion	Deep aspect of quadriceps tendon, then through patella to tibial tuberosity
Action	Extends leg at knee joint
Nerve	Femoral nerve (L2–L4)

Note: A few bundles of fibers from this muscle insert onto the upper part of the joint capsule of the knee. They probably draw the capsule superiorly during extension of the leg, preventing it from binding in the joint. They are called *articularis genus*.

Hip, thigh, and leg—anterior view

MUSCLES OF THE ANTERIOR THIGH

Hip and thigh—anterior view

1. Tensor fasciae latae
2. Iliotibial tract
3. Vastus lateralis (quadriceps femoris)
4. Vastus intermedius (quadriceps femoris)
5. Rectus femoris (cut) (quadriceps femoris)
6. Sartorius
7. Vastus medialis (quadriceps femoris)

BICEPS FEMORIS

(Part of hamstrings)

Hip and thigh—posterior view

Origin	Long head—ischial tuberosity, sacrotuberous ligament
	Short head—linea aspera, lateral supracondylar ridge, lateral intermuscular septum
Insertion	Lateral side of head of fibula and lateral condyle of tibia
Action	Flexes leg at knee joint, long head also extends thigh at hip joint

Nerve	Long head—tibial part of sciatic nerve (S1–S3)
	Short head—common peroneal part of sciatic nerve (L5, S1, S2)

Note: During walking or running the hamstrings are used to slow down the leg at the end of its swing and prevent the trunk from flexing at the hip. They are susceptible to being strained by resisting the momentum of these body parts.

SEMITENDINOSUS
(Part of hamstrings)

Hip and thigh—posterior view

Origin	Ischial tuberosity	**Nerve**	Tibial portion of sciatic nerve (L5, S1, S2)
Insertion	Medial surface of shaft of tibia		
Action	Flexes and slightly medially rotates leg at knee joint after flexion, extends thigh at hip joint		

Note: See note on biceps femoris and relationships section on sartorius.

SEMIMEMBRANOSUS

(Part of hamstrings)

Hip and thigh—posterior view

Origin	Ischial tuberosity	**Nerve**	Tibial portion of sciatic nerve (L5, S1, S2)
Insertion	Posterior part of medial condyle of tibia		
Action	Flexes and slightly medially rotates leg at knee joint after flexion, extends thigh at hip joint	Note: See note on biceps femoris.	

HAMSTRING MUSCLES

Hip and thigh—posterior view

1. Sciatic nerve
2. Quadratus femoris
3. Biceps femoris
4. Semimembranosus
5. Semitendinosus

6. Tibial nerve
7. Common peroneal nerve

Note: The common peroneal nerve is exposed to compression and damage as it passes over the head of the fibula.

The quadratus femoris, a lateral rotator, is included for reference.

GRACILIS

Origin	Lower margin of body and inferior ramus of pubis
Insertion	Upper part of medial surface of shaft of tibia
Action	Adducts thigh at hip joint and flexes leg at knee joint; with leg flexed assists in medial rotation
Nerve	Obturator nerve (L3, L4)

Note: See relationships section on sartorius.

Hip and thigh—anterior view

PECTINEUS

Origin	Pectineal line on superior ramus of pubis
Insertion	From lesser trochanter to linea aspera of femur
Action	Flexes and adducts thigh at hip joint, medially rotates thigh
Nerve	Femoral nerve (L2–L4), (sometimes a branch of obturator nerve)

Hip and thigh—anterior view

ADDUCTOR LONGUS

Hip and thigh—posterior view

Origin   Anterior of body of pubis

Insertion   Medial lip of linea aspera

Action   Adducts thigh, assists in medial rotation

Nerve   Obturator nerve (L3, L4)

ADDUCTOR BREVIS

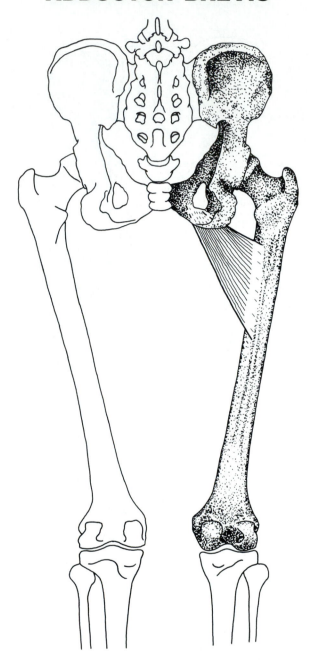

Hip and thigh—posterior view

Origin   Outer surface of inferior ramus of pubis

Insertion   From below lesser trochanter to linea aspera and into proximal part of linea aspera

Action   Adducts thigh, assists in medial rotation

Nerve   Obturator nerve (L3, L4)

ADDUCTOR MAGNUS

Hip and thigh—posterior view

Origin	Inferior ramus of pubis, and ramus and lower part of tuberosity of ischium	**Action**	Adducts thigh, assists in medial rotation
Insertion	Linea aspera, adductor tubercle of femur	**Nerve**	Obturator nerve (L3, L4), sciatic nerve

HIP FLEXORS AND ADDUCTORS

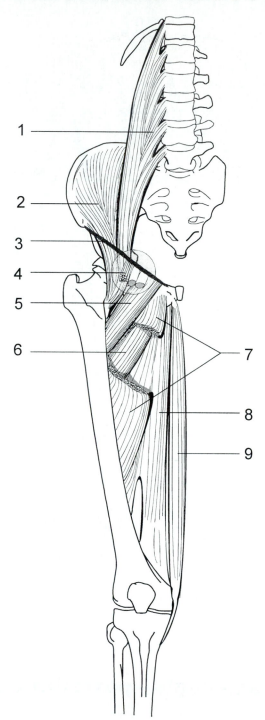

1
2
3
4
5
6
7
8
9

Hip and thigh—anterior view

1. Psoas major
2. Iliacus
3. Inguinal ligament
4. Femoral nerve, vein, artery
5. Pectineus

6. Adductor brevis
7. Adductor longus (cut)
8. Adductor magnus
9. Gracilis

CHAPTER NINE
MUSCLES OF THE LEG AND FOOT

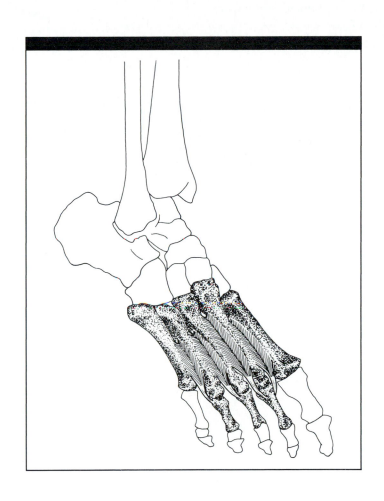

TIBIALIS ANTERIOR

Origin   Lateral condyle of tibia, upper half of
               lateral surface of tibia, interosseous
               membrane

Insertion Medial side and plantar surface of
               medial cuneiform bone, and base of
               first metatarsal bone

Action   Dorsiflexes foot at ankle joint, inverts
               (supinates) foot

Nerve   Deep peroneal nerve (L4, L5, S1)

Leg—anterolateral view

EXTENSOR HALLUCIS LONGUS

Origin	Middle half of anterior surface of fibula and interosseous membrane
Insertion	Base of distal phalanx of great toe
Action	Extends great toe, dorsiflexes and inverts (supinates) foot
Nerve	Deep peroneal nerve (L4, L5, S1)

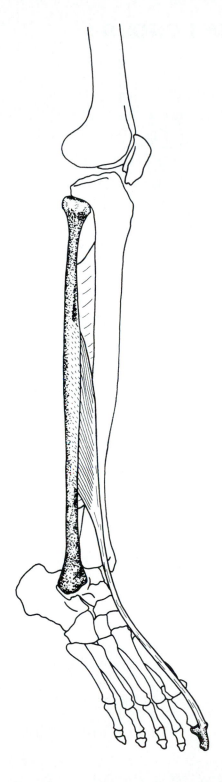

Leg—anterolateral view

EXTENSOR DIGITORUM LONGUS

Leg—anterolateral view

Foot—anterolateral view

Origin	Upper two-thirds of anterior surface of fibula, interosseous membrane, lateral condyle of tibia
Insertion	Along dorsal surface of four lateral toes, and then to bases of middle and distal phalanges
Action	Extends toes, dorsiflexes foot at ankle, everts foot
Nerve	Deep peroneal nerve (L4, L5, S1)

Note: The lower lateral part of this muscle makes a separate insertion onto the dorsal surface of the fifth metatarsal and is called *peroneus tertius*.

PERONEUS TERTIUS

(Lower lateral part of extensor digitorum longus)

Origin	Lower third of anterior surface of fibula and interosseous membrane
Insertion	Dorsal surface of base of fifth metatarsal bone
Action	Dorsiflexes and everts foot
Nerve	Deep peroneal nerve (L4, L5, S1)

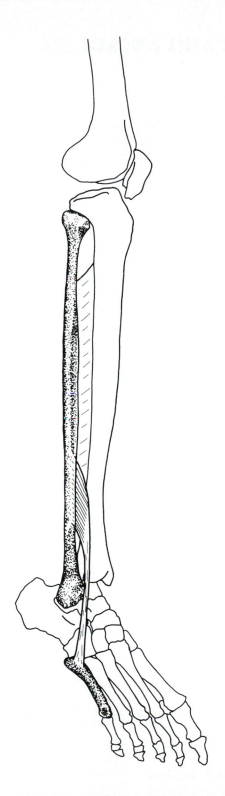

Leg—anterolateral view

ANTERIOR AND LATERAL LEG MUSCLES

Leg—anterolateral view

1. Peroneus longus
2. Peroneus brevis
3. Peroneus tertius
4. Tibialis anterior

5. Extensor retinaculum
6. Extensor hallucis longus
7. Extensor digitorum longus
8. Extensor digitorum brevis

GASTROCNEMIUS

(Part of triceps surae)

Origin
Lateral head—lateral condyle and posterior surface of femur

Medial head—popliteal surface of femur above medial condyle

Insertion
Posterior surface of the calcaneus

Action
Plantar flexes foot, flexes leg at knee

Nerve
Tibial nerve (S1, S2)

Leg—posterior view

SOLEUS

(Part of triceps surae)

Origin	Posterior surface of the tibia (soleal line), upper third of posterior surface of fibula, fibrous arch between tibia and fibula
Insertion	Posterior surface of the calcaneus
Action	Plantar flexes foot
Nerve	Tibial nerve (S1, S2)

Leg—posterior view

PLANTARIS

Origin	Lateral supracondylar ridge of femur, oblique popliteal ligament
Insertion	Posterior surface of the calcaneus
Action	Plantar flexes foot, flexes leg
Nerve	Tibial nerve (L4, L5, S1)

Leg—posterior view

MUSCLES OF THE CALF

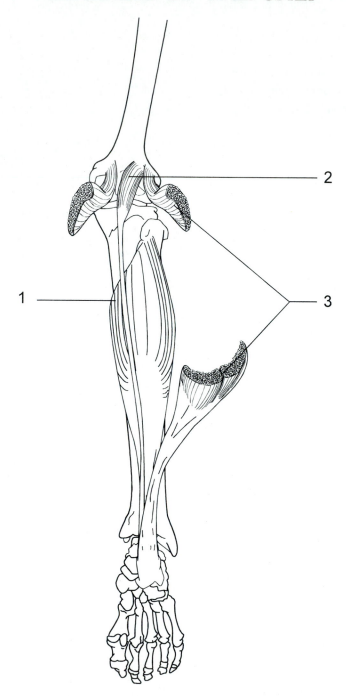

Leg—posterior view

1. Soleus
2. Plantaris
3. Gastrocnemius (cut)

Leg—posterior view

POPLITEUS

Origin	Lateral surface of lateral condyle of femur
Insertion	Upper part of posterior surface of tibia
Action	Rotates leg medially, flexes leg
Nerve	Tibial nerve (L4, L5, S1)

Note: Stern* contends that this muscle stabilizes the knee by preventing lateral rotation of the tibia during jmedial rotation of the thigh while the foot is planted.

*References:

Agur, AMR.: Grant's Atlas of Anatomy, 9th ed. Williams and Wilkins, Baltimore, 1991.
Stern, JT: Essentials of Gross Anatomy, F. A. Davis Company, Philadelphia, 1988.

FLEXOR HALLUCIS LONGUS

Origin   Lower two-thirds of posterior surface
                    of shaft of fibula, posterior
                    intermuscular septum, interosseous
                    membrane
Insertion   Base of distal phalanx of great toe
Action   Flexes distal phalanx of great toe,
                    assists in plantar flexing foot, inverts
                    foot
Nerve   Tibial nerve (L5, S1, S2)

Leg—posterior view

FLEXOR DIGITORUM LONGUS

Foot—plantar view

Origin	Medial part of posterior surface of tibia
Insertion	Bases of distal phalanges of second, third, fourth, and fifth toes
Action	Flexes distal phalanges of lateral four toes, assists in plantar flexing foot, inverts foot
Nerve	Tibial nerve (L5, S1)

Leg—posterior view

TIBIALIS POSTERIOR

Foot—plantar view

Origin	Lateral part of posterior surface of tibia, interosseous membrane, proximal half of posterior surface of fibula
Insertion	Tuberosity of navicular bone, cuboid, cuneiforms, second, third, and fourth metatarsals, sustentaculum tali of calcaneus
Action	Plantar flexes, inverts foot
Nerve	Tibial nerve (L5, S1)

Leg—posterior view

DEEP POSTERIOR LEG MUSCLES

Leg—posterior view

1. Popliteus
2. Tibialis posterior
2a. Tendon of tibialis posterior

3. Flexor hallucis longus (cut)
4. Flexor digitorum longus (cut)
5. Medial malleolus

PERONEUS LONGUS

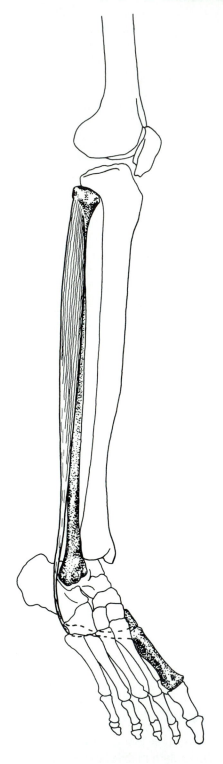

Foot—plantar view

Origin	Upper two-thirds of lateral surface of fibula
Insertion	Lateral side of medial cuneiform, base of first metatarsal
Action	Plantar flexes, everts foot
Nerve	Superficial peroneal nerve (L4, L5, S1)

Leg—anterolateral view

PERONEUS BREVIS

Origin   Lower two-thirds of lateral surface of fibula

Insertion   Lateral side of base of fifth metatarsal bone

Action   Everts, plantar flexes foot

Nerve   Superficial peroneal nerve (L4, L5, S1)

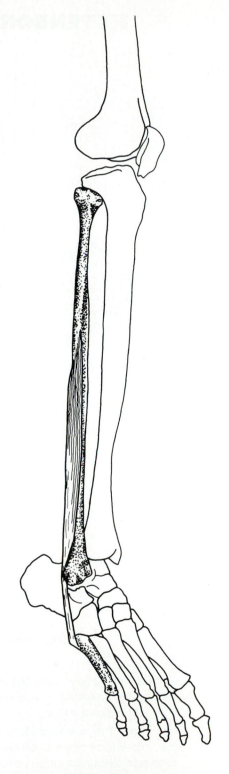

Leg—anterolateral view

EXTENSOR DIGITORUM BREVIS

Foot—anterolateral view

Origin   Anterior and lateral surfaces of
                  calcaneus, lateral talocalcaneal
                  ligament, inferior extensor retinaculum

Insertion   Into base of proximal phalanx of great
                  toe, into lateral sides of tendons of
                  extensor digitorum longus of second,
                  third, and fourth toes

Action   Extends the four toes

Nerve   Deep peroneal nerve (L5, S1)

ABDUCTOR HALLUCIS
(First layer)

Foot—plantar view

Origin	Tuberosity of calcaneus, flexor retinaculum, plantar aponeurosis
Insertion	Medial side of base of proximal phalanx of great toe
Action	Abducts great toe
Nerve	Medial plantar nerve (L4, L5)

Note: The muscles of the sole of the foot can be divided into four layers (from superficial to deep):

First layer—abductor hallucis, flexor digitorum brevis, abductor digiti minimi

Second layer—quadratus plantae, lumbricales (tendons of flexor hallucis longus and flexor digitorum longus pass through this layer)

Third layer—flexor hallucis brevis, adductor hallucis, flexor digiti minimi brevis

Fourth layer—interossei (tendons of tibialis posterior and peroneus longus pass through this layer)

FLEXOR DIGITORUM BREVIS
(First layer)

Foot—plantar view

Origin	Tuberosity of calcaneus, plantar aponeurosis	**Action**	Flexes proximal phalanges and extends distal phalanges of second through fifth toes
Insertion	Sides of middle phalanges of second to fifth toes	**Nerve**	Medial plantar nerve (L4, L5)

ABDUCTOR DIGITI MINIMI
(First layer)

Foot—plantar view

Origin	Tuberosity of calcaneus, plantar aponeurosis	**Action**	Abducts fifth toe
		Nerve	Lateral plantar nerve (S1, S2)
Insertion	Lateral side of proximal phalanx of fifth toe		

QUADRATUS PLANTAE

(Second layer)

Foot—plantar view

Origin	Medial head—medial surface of calcaneus	**Action**	Flexes terminal phalanges of second through fifth toes
	Lateral head—lateral border of inferior surface of calcaneus	**Nerve**	Lateral plantar nerve (S1, S2)
Insertion	Lateral margin of tendon of flexor digitorum longus		

LUMBRICALES

(Second layer)

Foot—plantar view

Origin	Tendons of flexor digitorum longus	**Nerve**	First lumbricalis—medial plantar nerve (L4, L5)
Insertion	Dorsal surfaces of proximal phalanges		Second through fifth lumbricales— lateral plantar nerve (S1, S2)
Action	Flex proximal phalanges of second through fifth toes		

FLEXOR HALLUCIS BREVIS
(Third layer)

Foot—plantar view

Origin	Cuboid bone, lateral cuneiform bone	**Action**	Flexes proximal phalanx of great toe
Insertion	Medial part—medial side of base of proximal phalanx of great toe	**Nerve**	Medial plantar nerve (L4, L5, S1)
	Lateral part—lateral side of base of proximal phalanx of great toe		

ADDUCTOR HALLUCIS
(Third layer)

Foot—plantar view

Origin

Oblique head—second, third, and fourth metatarsal bones, and sheath of peroneus longus tendon

Transverse head—plantar metatarsophalangeal ligaments of third, fourth, and fifth toes, and transverse metatarsal ligaments

Insertion

Lateral side of base of proximal phalanx of great toe

Action

Adducts great toe

Nerve

Lateral plantar nerve (S1, S2)

FLEXOR DIGITI MINIMI BREVIS
(Third layer)

Foot—plantar view

Origin	Base of fifth metatarsal, sheath of peroneus longus tendon	**Action**	Flexes proximal phalanx of fifth toe
Insertion	Lateral side of base of proximal phalanx of fifth toe	**Nerve**	Lateral plantar nerve (S1, S2)

DORSAL INTEROSSEI
(Fourth layer; four muscles)

Foot—anterolateral view

Origin   Adjacent sides of metatarsal bones

Insertion   Bases of proximal phalanges
First—medial side of proximal phalanx of second toe
Second, third, fourth—lateral sides of proximal phalanges of second, third, and fourth toes

Action   Abduct toes, flex proximal phalanges

Nerve   Lateral plantar nerve (S1, S2)

PLANTAR INTEROSSEI
(Fourth layer; three muscles)

Foot—plantar view

Origin	Bases and medial sides of third, fourth, and fifth metatarsal bones	**Action**	Adduct toes, flex proximal phalanges
Insertion	Medial sides of bases of proximal phalanges of same toes	**Nerve**	Lateral plantar nerve (S1, S2)

Alphabetical Listing Of Muscles

Index